Urban America

OPPOSING VIEWPOINTS®

Laura K. Egendorf, *Book Editor*

Bruce Glassman, *Vice President*
Bonnie Szumski, *Publisher*
Helen Cothran, *Managing Editor*

**OPPOSING
VIEWPOINTS®
SERIES**

GREENHAVEN PRESS
An imprint of Thomson Gale, a part of The Thomson Corporation

THOMSON
GALE

Detroit • New York • San Francisco • San Diego • New Haven, Conn.
Waterville, Maine • London • Munich

LIBRARY OF CONGRESS CATALOGING-IN-PUBLICATION DATA
Urban America / Laura K. Egendorf, book editor.
p. cm. — (Opposing viewpoints series)
Includes bibliographical references and index.
ISBN 0-7377-2967-8 (lib. : alk. paper) — ISBN 0-7377-2968-6 (pbk. : alk. paper)
1. Cities and towns—United States. 2. Sociology, urban—United States. 3. Urban policy—United States. I. Egendorf, Laura K., 1973– . II. Series.
HT123.U724 2005
307.76'0973—dc22   2004060641

Printed in the United States of America

"Congress shall make no law. . .abridging the freedom of speech, or of the press."

First Amendment to the U.S. Constitution

The basic foundation of our democracy is the First Amendment guarantee of freedom of expression. The Opposing Viewpoints Series is dedicated to the concept of this basic freedom and the idea that it is more important to practice it than to enshrine it.

Contents

Chapter 3: How Can the Lives of Urban Children Be Improved?

Chapter 4: What Is the Future of Urban America?

Why Consider Opposing Viewpoints?

"The only way in which a human being can make some approach to knowing the whole of a subject is by hearing what can be said about it by persons of every variety of opinion and studying all modes in which it can be looked at by every character of mind. No wise man ever acquired his wisdom in any mode but this."

John Stuart Mill

In our media-intensive culture it is not difficult to find differing opinions. Thousands of newspapers and magazines and dozens of radio and television talk shows resound with differing points of view. The difficulty lies in deciding which opinion to agree with and which "experts" seem the most credible. The more inundated we become with differing opinions and claims, the more essential it is to hone critical reading and thinking skills to evaluate these ideas. Opposing Viewpoints books address this problem directly by presenting stimulating debates that can be used to enhance and teach these skills. The varied opinions contained in each book examine many different aspects of a single issue. While examining these conveniently edited opposing views, readers can develop critical thinking skills such as the ability to compare and contrast authors' credibility, facts, argumentation styles, use of persuasive techniques, and other stylistic tools. In short, the Opposing Viewpoints Series is an ideal way to attain the higher-level thinking and reading skills so essential in a culture of diverse and contradictory opinions.

In addition to providing a tool for critical thinking, Opposing Viewpoints books challenge readers to question their own strongly held opinions and assumptions. Most people form their opinions on the basis of upbringing, peer pressure, and personal, cultural, or professional bias. By reading carefully balanced opposing views, readers must directly confront new ideas as well as the opinions of those with whom they disagree. This is not to simplistically argue that everyone who reads opposing views will—or should— change his or her opinion. Instead, the series enhances readers' understanding of their own views by encouraging confrontation with opposing ideas. Careful examination of others' views can lead to the readers' understanding of the logical inconsistencies in their own opinions, perspective on why they hold an opinion, and the consideration of the possibility that their opinion requires further evaluation.

Evaluating Other Opinions

To ensure that this type of examination occurs, Opposing Viewpoints books present all types of opinions. Prominent spokespeople on different sides of each issue as well as well-known professionals from many disciplines challenge the reader. An additional goal of the series is to provide a forum for other, less known, or even unpopular viewpoints. The opinion of an ordinary person who has had to make the decision to cut off life support from a terminally ill relative, for example, may be just as valuable and provide just as much insight as a medical ethicist's professional opinion. The editors have two additional purposes in including these less known views. One, the editors encourage readers to respect others' opinions—even when not enhanced by professional credibility. It is only by reading or listening to and objectively evaluating others' ideas that one can determine whether they are worthy of consideration. Two, the inclusion of such viewpoints encourages the important critical thinking skill of objectively evaluating an author's credentials and bias. This evaluation will illuminate an author's reasons for taking a particular stance on an issue and will aid in readers' evaluation of the author's ideas.

It is our hope that these books will give readers a deeper understanding of the issues debated and an appreciation of the complexity of even seemingly simple issues when good and honest people disagree. This awareness is particularly important in a democratic society such as ours in which people enter into public debate to determine the common good. Those with whom one disagrees should not be regarded as enemies but rather as people whose views deserve careful examination and may shed light on one's own.

Thomas Jefferson once said that "difference of opinion leads to inquiry, and inquiry to truth." Jefferson, a broadly educated man, argued that "if a nation expects to be ignorant and free . . . it expects what never was and never will be." As individuals and as a nation, it is imperative that we consider the opinions of others and examine them with skill and discernment. The Opposing Viewpoints Series is intended to help readers achieve this goal.

David L. Bender and Bruno Leone,
Founders

Greenhaven Press anthologies primarily consist of previously published material taken from a variety of sources, including periodicals, books, scholarly journals, newspapers, government documents, and position papers from private and public organizations. These original sources are often edited for length and to ensure their accessibility for a young adult audience. The anthology editors also change the original titles of these works in order to clearly present the main thesis of each viewpoint and to explicitly indicate the opinion presented in the viewpoint. These alterations are made in consideration of both the reading and comprehension levels of a young adult audience. Every effort is made to ensure that Greenhaven Press accurately reflects the original intent of the authors included in this anthology.

Introduction

"The Progressive Era was marked by a radical growth in the extension and dominance of government in America's economic, social, and cultural life."

—Murray N. Rothbard, economist

"The turn of the [twenty-first] century has witnessed a new opening for a progressive renewal in American politics."

—Robert L. Borosage, codirector of the Campaign for America's Future, and Stanley B. Greenberg, cofounder of Democracy Corps

Life in modern urban America is beset by several problems, from poverty to a lack of affordable housing to crime. These problems are not new, however. After the Civil War, the United States became increasingly industrialized. With more Americans moving to cities, urban America—and its troubles—expanded. Workers in urban factories toiled in difficult conditions, working in unsafe environments for low wages; even children were not immune from the exploitation. In the waning years of the nineteenth century, a political movement known as the Progressive movement emerged. Its adherents spurred the passage of laws that improved the quality of life for many urban Americans. Progressivism faded away in the 1920s and 1930s, but many people in the past several years have called for a new progressivism, which again takes into account the social and economic concerns of city dwellers.

After the Civil War the United States entered an era nicknamed the "Gilded Age" by author and humorist Mark Twain. In his mind the glamour of industrial wealth covered a dark heart of political and economic corruption. Industrialization made some families extraordinarily wealthy, but that wealth came at the expense of average Americans, many of whom worked in the steel factories and other businesses that made those select families rich. Urban Americans in the late nineteenth century were further victimized by political corruption. Governments frequently operated at the behest of big business and neglected important public services.

It was in this environment that the Progressive movement grew. Progressives sought to limit the power of corporations in order to ensure that workers received better treatment and that the average city dweller could live in safe and clean housing. Progressives were especially concerned with urban children and sought laws that regulated child labor and guaranteed that all children received an education.

Women played an important role in the Progressive movement. Jane Addams spent much of her life working to improve housing and working conditions for Chicagoans. Her Hull House provided key services to the city's immigrant population, including medical care and vocational training. She also lobbied for laws to protect urban workers. The General Federation of Women's Clubs supported many of the same goals as Addams and also backed legislation for the eight-hour workday, the regulation of child labor, and compulsory school attendance.

Some politicians during this time also sought to better the lives of urban Americans. While mayors were elected in Detroit, San Francisco, and other cities on platforms that promised better city services and stricter housing codes, the Progressive movement was strongest in Wisconsin. Craig Gilbert, writing for the *Milwaukee Journal-Sentinel*, notes that Wisconsin progressivism, which was led by Robert "Fighting Bob" La Follette, "featured activism, reform, a more expansive notion of government services, . . . and a regulatory agenda aimed at curbing the power of 'monied interests.'" On the federal level the government established the U.S. Children's Bureau in 1912. Congress passed the Keating-Owens Act, the first federal law regulating child labor, four years later, although the Supreme Court declared the legislation unconstitutional the following year.

Certainly the Progressive movement did not succeed in achieving all its goals, partly because it could not fully break corporate control of government. However, the creation of the graduated income tax, which ensured that the wealthy would pay their fair share, and the implementation of government supervision of the food and drug industry (a result of Upton Sinclair's book *The Jungle*, which explored in shocking detail the unsafe and unsanitary conditions in Chicago's meatpacking industry) are indications that the Progressives accomplished a great deal before the movement faded away between the two world wars.

The end of the twentieth century and the beginning of the twenty-first has brought a return of progressive politics. As was the case a hundred years ago, the followers of this new Progressive movement believe that the government must tackle urban America's economic and social problems. In his commentary, "A Movement for Economic Security in an Age of Change," Roger Hickey, the codirector of the Campaign for America's Future, declares that this new era of progressivism must target the special interests that influence government, echoing progressives during the Gilded Age. He also argues, "Public policy should expand opportunity and close the growing wage and income gaps in the United States." Hickey further suggests that the revitalization of urban America must be a priority for all levels of government. In the introduction to their book *The Next Agenda: Blueprint for a New Progressive Movement*, Robert L. Borosage and Stanley B. Greenberg, codirector of the Campaign for America's Future and cofounder of Democracy Corps, respectively, call for the improvement of America's schools, an objective shared with early women progressives. Like Hickey, the authors also support raising wages and investing in America's cities.

A return to progressive politics is not seen by everyone as the best way to better the lives of urban American, however. Supporters of free-market solutions assert that government laws regulating labor, for example, are not always effective and can be economically and politically burdensome. In his essay, "The Progressive Era and the Family," economist Murray N. Rothbard declares that during the earlier progressive era, "the entire American polity—from economics to urban planning to medicine to social work to the licensing of professions to the ideology of intellectuals—was transformed from a roughly laissez-faire system based on individual rights to one of state planning and control."

As long as problems persist in America's cities, politicians, organizations, and concerned citizens will continue to look for solutions, perhaps those offered by the new Progressive movement. In *Opposing Viewpoints: Urban America*, the authors address the issues facing the nation's cities in the following chapters: What Problems Is Urban America Facing? What Government Programs Would Improve Urban America? How Can the Lives of Urban Children Be Improved? What Is the Future of Urban America? The arguments offered by these contributors show that the past, present, and future of America's cities have a great deal in common.

What Problems Is Urban America Facing?

Chapter Preface

When examining the challenges that face urban Americans, it is important to consider how economic and social problems affect city residents' lives on a day-to-day basis. One of the biggest challenges of urban life is driving. Rush hour traffic and easily riled drivers are among the factors that make city driving an often unpleasant experience. Another factor that makes driving a problem in urban America is the poor quality of the nation's roads. Potholes and cracks on city streets and poorly paved freeways cost urban Americans millions of dollars in car repair costs each year.

A significant proportion of city streets and freeways are in poor condition. According to The Road Information Program (TRIP), a nonprofit organization that researches and evaluates data on highway transportation issues, "One out of four (25 percent) of the nation's major metropolitan roads—interstates, freeways and other principal arterial routes—have pavements that are in poor condition. Pavement conditions on the nation's major urban roads and highways have worsened in each year since 1998." TRIP further notes that some metropolitan areas are especially beleaguered by poor roads. Southern California, with its extensive freeway system and limited public transportation, has particularly lousy roads—66 percent of the roads in Los Angeles, 60 percent in San Diego, and 42 percent in Riverside–San Bernardino are in undesirable condition.

With the amount of time many drivers spend on city roads and freeways, commuting to and from work and running errands, it is not surprising that driving through potholes and over uneven and cracked asphalt causes significant damage to automobiles. TRIP estimates that deteriorating roads cost urban Americans an average of $396 per year, with Los Angeles–area drivers averaging $706. As the number of drivers increases every year, the economic costs associated with the poor condition of U.S. roads will continue to rise.

This problem is likely to persist unless federal, state, and local governments provide more funding. In May 2003 Missouri senator Jim Talent introduced a bill, "Build America

Bonds," that would provide $50 million in bonds to address America's transportation needs, including improving city streets. In a press release on his Web site, Talent notes, "By building and repairing our roads, bridges, railways, runways, transit systems and ports we will create jobs now and enable economic recovery for the future." Talent's legislation became part of another Senate transportation bill, which as of July 2004 was being considered by the House of Representatives as an amendment to its own bill on highway funding; no further action has been taken. A study by the Department of Transportation (DOT) points out that an increase in funding is vital if America's roads are to show any significant improvement; according to the DOT's report, the overall expenditure of $11.1 billion per year falls far short of the $14.6 billion needed to keep urban streets at their current condition and the $18 billion that must be spent each year if the roads are to be repaved and repaired.

The condition of urban America's roads is one of the many problems facing American cities. As cities are the home to millions of Americans, the quality of life in the nation's metropolises is a matter worth serious consideration. In the following chapter the authors analyze the state of urban America.

"The concentration and isolation of poor people in central cities have worsened during the past few decades."

Urban Poverty Is a Serious Problem

Charles C. Euchner and Stephen J. McGovern

In the following viewpoint Charles C. Euchner and Stephen J. McGovern contend that poverty is a significant problem in American cities, especially for minorities. According to the authors, the percentage of blacks and Latinos living in high-poverty urban neighborhoods has risen significantly since the 1970s. They further assert that racial discrimination and segregation worsen the economic problems of urban minorities, leading to isolation from the rest of American society. Euchner is the executive director of the Rappaport Institute for Greater Boston at Harvard University's Kennedy School of Government, and McGovern is an assistant professor of political science at Haverford College in Pennsylvania.

As you read, consider the following questions:
1. According to the authors why is it difficult for urban residents to find good jobs?
2. What proportion of residents in extremely high-poverty neighborhoods are minorities, as stated by the authors?
3. What happened to the inner cities once middle-class blacks departed, in Euchner and McGovern's opinion?

*P*overty exists all over the United States. Is it more problematic in cities?

Poverty pervades all regions of the United States and affects racial and ethnic groups. However, in recent decades poverty has become increasingly concentrated in urban neighborhoods, especially those in older, industrial cities. The political scientist Paul Jargowsky found that the number of people living in high-poverty neighborhoods almost doubled between 1970 and 1990, from 1.9 million to 3.7 million. The problem fell disproportionately upon blacks and Latinos; 34 percent of poor blacks and 22 percent of poor Latinos lived in high-poverty neighborhoods in 1990, compared to only 6 percent of poor whites. Many U.S. cities witnessed a dramatic increase in concentrations of poverty among blacks and Latinos. In Detroit, for instance, only 11.3 percent of blacks lived in high-poverty neighborhoods in 1970; by 1990, that figure had ballooned to 53.9 percent. Increases in the concentration of poverty among blacks during the same period was substantial in many other cities as well (e.g., 27 percent in New York City, 22 percent in Pittsburgh, and 21 percent in Chicago). For Latinos, the increases were similarly grim (e.g., 48 percent in Philadelphia and 34 percent in Detroit).

The Poor Are Isolated

The growing concentration of poverty in American cities undermines the prospects of individuals living in impoverished neighborhoods. To start, the physical isolation makes it far more challenging for residents to find and hold good jobs. Obtaining access to employment opportunities on the other side of the city or in an outlying suburb may be difficult or impossible because of the unavailability of public transportation or the high cost of commuting by automobile. Information about job openings may be extremely limited because of the lack of social networks linking inner-city neighborhoods with more prosperous parts of the metropolitan area.

Restricted access to good job opportunities is not necessarily a new problem for inner-city residents. But what is relatively new, according to the sociologist William Julius Wilson, is the outmigration of many middle-class residents, who

18

are no longer trapped in inner-city neighborhoods by pervasive racial discrimination. As nonpoor blacks and Latinos move to more affluent areas, they leave behind the poorest of the poor, who find it increasingly difficult to sustain community organizations and institutions. As schools, churches, and clubs decline, the social organization of inner-city neighborhoods breaks down, which in turn leads to a disintegration of public order. Drug and alcohol abuse, crime, and other forms of dysfunctional behavior become commonplace, all of which further impede the life chances of neighborhood residents. Young people are particularly vulnerable to the temptations of the deviant culture of joblessness and chronic poverty.

In sum, the concentration and isolation of poor people in central cities have worsened during the past few decades, with grave consequences not just for the immediate victims of poverty but for all citizens in metropolitan areas. Poverty is arguably the most serious urban dilemma today, because from it flow so many other social, economic, and political problems. . . .

The Racial Element of Poverty

Is race a useful way to understand poverty in the city?

[Economist] Gunner Myrdal called race a unique "American dilemma." Slavery, the Civil War, Reconstruction, and Jim Crow [discriminatory laws] burnished the national psyche with race. Blacks came to the United States as property in chains, knowing that the system was designed specifically to exploit and exclude them. Other groups in this nation of immigrants came of their own will and knew they could make a place for themselves and their children within a generation or two.

Every newcomer to the United States has experienced some form of discrimination. Germans, Irish, Italians, Greeks, Chinese, and Vietnamese confronted epithets, exclusion, and even violence as they settled into American life. But most groups eventually begin to get "white" status. Established whites become willing to accept them as neighbors, coworkers, and even mates. They begin to identify themselves as white on census forms. But blacks have faced a more stubborn resistance. As [political scientist] Andrew Hacker notes, the United States "has chosen to reject the idea of a graduated spectrum, and has instead fashioned a rigid bifurcation." One is either white or not. The consequences are devastating for blacks. "Black Americans come from the least-known continent, the most exotic, the one remotest from the American experience. Among the burdens blacks bear is the stigma of 'the savage' the proximity to lesser primates. . . . No other racial or national origin is seen as having so pervasive a personality or character."

Statistics attest to the importance of race in American life. Blacks comprise 12 percent of the U.S. population but 55 percent of those who live in poverty for a long time and 60 percent of those who get welfare benefits for a long time. Almost seven eighths of the residents in extremely high-poverty neighborhoods are members of minority groups. Minorities in cities are much more likely to live in such communities as whites. In 1990, 14 percent of the black population and 9.4 percent of the Hispanic population residing in cities lived in extremely poor neighborhoods, compared to just 1 percent of the white population. Even when blacks gain the wherewithal to escape their racially segregated communities and move to white communities, whites leave those communities.

Even when blacks succeed, they face barriers to full participation in every walk of American life. With all other factors "held constant," blacks still face pervasive discrimination in getting a job, securing an apartment, obtaining a home mortgage, gaining acceptance in a neighborhood, getting home owner and other forms of insurance, winning admission to schools and universities, and gaining access to a wide variety of public accommodations from retail outlets to restaurants to taxi service.

Segregation Worsens Poverty

How important is segregation to the perpetuation of poverty?

Segregation intensifies the experience of poverty in minority communities. Isolation from job, health care, education, and other opportunities not only hurts the individuals involved but also undermines the development of community. In their book *American Apartheid*, Douglas Massey and Nancy Denton consider a hypothetical American city with 128,000 residents and divided into sixteen neighborhoods. The city's 96,000 whites (three quarters of the population) experience a 10 percent poverty rate, while the city's 32,000 blacks (one quarter of the population) experience a 20 percent poverty rate. All of these figures are roughly representative of the American urban experience.

If the city experienced no segregation, both blacks and whites would live in neighborhoods with 12.5 percent poverty rates. If four of the city's 16 neighborhoods were exclusively white, the poverty rate in the white areas would be 10 percent and the poverty rate in the other areas would be 13.3 percent. If half of the city's 16 sections were exclusively white, the mixed neighborhoods would experience a 15 percent poverty rate.

When racial segregation is reinforced by class segregation—as it almost always is—the results are even more devastating. When both black and white poor are confined to half of the city's neighborhoods, the intensity of that poverty dramatically increases. Poor blacks living in cities with low racial segregation and class segregation experience a neighborhood poverty rate of 28.3 percent. High racial segregation plus class segregation produces black neighborhoods with 35 percent poverty rates. A city completely segregated by race and class produces 40 percent poverty rates in the black neighborhoods. The situation would be more extreme if the exclusively white sections of the segregated city had 5 percent poverty rates, with a greater percentage of whites living in poverty in mixed neighborhoods, as is usually the case. In a city of half-white neighborhoods and half-mixed neighborhoods, the mixed neighborhoods would have a 20 percent poverty rate. Increase the black poverty rate from 20 to 30 percent, and the rates of poverty for the three black neighborhoods are 35, 45, and 60 percent.

That kind of concentration of poverty in black neighborhoods produces devastating effects on social structures and mores. Intensely poor neighborhoods are much more vulnerable to downturns in the economy. As noted above, a "culture of poverty" often results when the poorest of the poor are isolated from mainstream society.

In addition, poor minority neighborhoods are more likely to face a "self-perpetuating spiral of neighborhood decline." According to a study by the U.S. Department of Housing and Urban Development, once 3 to 6 percent of a neighborhood's buildings are abandoned, "investment psychology becomes so depressed that reversal of the abandonment process is impossible without major external intervention." That "tipping point" is likely to be reached with rates of neighborhood poverty near 50 percent.

Hunger Among the Urban Poor

According to the U.S. Department of Agriculture, 1.6 million New Yorkers, or the equivalent of the population of Philadelphia, suffer from "food insecurity," which is a fancy way of saying they don't have enough to eat. Some are the people who come in at night and clean those skyscrapers that glitter along the river. Some pour coffee and take care of the aged parents of the people who live in those buildings. The American Dream for the well-to-do grows from the bowed backs of the working poor.

Anna Quindlen, *Newsweek*, December 1, 2003.

How can we measure levels of segregation? What do those measures show?

Blacks did not always live apart from whites, but cities and suburbs have become intensely and intricately segregated in the twentieth century. Using an "isolation index," Massey and Denton have tracked the degree of neighborhood integration throughout the twentieth century. The index measures the makeup of neighborhoods where blacks live; a score of 100 percent indicates that all blacks live in completely black areas; a value under 50 percent indicates that a black is more likely to have whites than blacks as neighbors. In three quarters of all American cities in 1890, the index was 10 percent—meaning that the typical black lived in a 90 percent white neighborhood. By 1930, the index for Northern industrial cities had increased to 31.7 percent. By 1970, the index for the thirty metropolitan areas with the largest black populations was 69.3 percent, and in 1980 it was 63.5 percent.

Much of the isolation is owed to suburbanization, which has produced white and black flight from the cities. The isolation index for blacks was 72.9 percent in cities and 39.7 percent in suburbs. Massey and Denton conclude: "Ironically, within a large, diverse, and highly mobile post-industrial society such as the United States, blacks living in the heart of the ghetto are among the most isolated people on earth."

The Impact of the Black Middle Class

But surely many blacks have experienced great progress as a result of the Civil Rights Movement. How can that progress of the growing black middle class be squared with the extreme isolation?

The Civil Rights Movement created unprecedented opportunities for blacks in the United States. For the first time in American history, blacks were guaranteed the rights to use basic public accommodations and to vote as a result of the Civil Rights Act of 1964 and the Voting Rights Act of 1965. They had the right to obtain shelter without discrimination as a result of the Housing Act of 1968. As a result of the Nixon Administration's so-called Philadelphia Plan, the forerunner of affirmative action, blacks had greater access to corporate and government jobs. Blacks earned college degrees in record numbers. At least some suburbs, usually right on the city's outskirts, opened to blacks for the first time. To be sure, most communities still practiced some subtle—and some not-so-subtle—forms of racial discrimination. But opportunities for upward mobility opened up for many blacks.

One result was the rise of the black middle class. Incomes rose. Blacks dramatically increased their numbers in the professions as well as in middle-class jobs that provide a steady if unspectacular living, such as police officers, electricians, bank tellers, and medical workers. Black women did especially well. (Employers seemed to prefer women to men among blacks because they are considered more accommodating.)

Between 1970 and 1990, the income distribution of blacks shifted from a classic pyramid with gradually smaller segments in the higher salary brackets. The new distribution had a bigger base, with more poor people, and a more even distribution of the upper income brackets. That is significant, as Andrew Hacker notes, because it signals "a separation of better-off blacks from those at the lowest level." Overall, black incomes remained steady, but the distribution changed to isolate poor blacks.

Middle-class blacks left the inner city for better economic opportunities, better schools, and the open spaces of the suburbs. This exodus took away some of the major supports of the neighborhood social structure in the city. Churches, political organizations, schools, and business groups all suffered from the loss of leadership and resources. Perhaps even more harmful was the loss of the moral authority of the departed middle class. Some of the most devastated areas became devoid of mainstream ideas and practices.

William Julius Wilson's book *The Truly Disadvantaged* traces the development of the underclass in America's cities. Wilson collected data from seventy-seven subdivisions of Chicago in 1970 and 1980. In 1970, only eight of these communities had poverty rates of 30 percent or more and only one had a poverty rate of 40 percent or more. Six of these communities moved from a high to an extreme poverty rate in a decade. One major reason for this more intense poverty is that 151,000 nonpoor blacks left these communities during that fateful decade. Nationally, the number of blacks living in the suburbs increased from 3.38 million in 1960 to 8.2 million in 1985. By 1989, 27 percent of all blacks lived in suburbs. These blacks had comprised the stable working class in the neighborhoods. After 1980, they were gone.

The Irony of Integration

How does segregation of groups affect economic mobility? Are the effects always negative?

The isolation of racial and ethnic groups has contradictory effects. On the one hand, segregation isolates minorities from a wide range of opportunities. On the other hand, segregation engenders economic and social diversity within racial or ethnic communities. In black urban communities before the Civil Rights Movement, people of all classes lived side by side. The preacher lived next door to the garbage man, the beautician next to the accountant, the teacher next to the maid. The proximity of diverse groups created a dynamic situation where people went their own ways but came to support each other in numerous ways. Black communities from Atlanta to the Los Angeles community of Watts, from Birmingham to American Beach, Florida, developed complex systems of mutuality that sustained generations of blacks from Reconstruction to the Civil Rights Movement. The most important consequence of segregation was the role model effect. Educated, upper-class families demonstrated a better way of life for the striving factory worker or janitor. The children of diverse families went to school and church together.

Ironically, when civil rights laws of the 1960s and 1970s forced whites to open up to black patronage, black businesses and communities suffered. In a study of the demise of the community of American Beach, Florida, Russ Rymer writes:

> Integration became the greatest opening of a domestic market in American history, but the windfall went in only one direction, with predictable, if unforeseen, results: the whole economic skeleton of the black community, so painfully erected in the face of exclusion and injustice, collapsed as that exclusion was rescinded. In this way, integration wiped out or humbled an important echelon of the black community—the non-clergy leadership class that had fought so hard for civil rights and was needed to show the way to pragmatic prosperity. Today's black professionals haven't replaced the old black entrepreneurs, because the money they bring home is earned almost exclusively from white-run companies. In the past, black wealth was generated out of the black community. Money entered at the bottom of the community and worked its way up, binding the classes together in mutual dependence and a linked destiny. White business sundered that connection by inserting itself between the black professional and black consumer classes.

Black neighborhoods lost their professional elites, their savings, and their consumer dollars to the larger, white-dominated system.

"By a sizeable number of indicators, there have been measurable improvements in conditions in high-poverty neighborhoods since 1990."

Urban Poverty Is Declining

G. Thomas Kingsley and Kathryn L.S. Pettit

The number of people living in high-poverty urban neighborhoods is declining, G. Thomas Kingsley and Kathryn L.S. Pettit claim in the following viewpoint. According to Kingsley and Pettit, poor urban Americans are increasingly living in neighborhoods where poverty is less concentrated. Furthermore, they contend that the education and employment status of urban Americans in high-poverty areas is improving, an indication that the overall condition of the urban poor is better. Kingsley and Pettit are the director and deputy director, respectively, of the National Neighborhood Indicators Partnership.

As you read, consider the following questions:
1. How many Americans lived in high-poverty neighborhoods in 2000, according to the authors?
2. As explained by Kingsley and Pettit, how are levels of concentrated poverty determined?
3. According to the authors, what was the percentage of households in high-poverty neighborhoods that received public assistance?

The data show that the 1990s brought a sharp reversal In the poverty concentration trend. . . . The most pronounced change was at the high end of the spectrum. The share of metropolitan poor who live in extreme-poverty tracts, which had jumped from 13 to 17 percent in the 1980s, dropped all the way back to 12 percent in 2000. The share in the 30–40 percent range stayed the same over the decade, but putting these two categories together, the share in high-poverty neighborhoods increased from 25 percent in 1980 to 31 percent in 1990 and then fell back to 26 percent in 2000.

One-quarter of America's metropolitan poor lived in low-poverty neighborhoods (rates in the 0–10 percent range) in 2000, not much different than the figure for 1990. The compensating increases occurred in the two intermediate categories. The share of all poor people in tracts with poverty rates in the 20–30 percent range increased from 18 to 21 percent and that in the 10–20 percent range from 27 to 29 percent.

The overall poverty rate in U.S. metropolitan areas remained virtually constant (11–12 percent range) from 1980 to 2000, but with increasing total population, the absolute number of poor people increased from 19.3 million in 1980 to 23.1 million in 1990 and 25.8 million in 2000. The number living in high-poverty neighborhoods increased from 4.9 million in 1980 to 7.1 million in 1990, but then declined to 6.7 million at century's end. In contrast, the number of poor people in tracts with poverty rates ranging from 10 to 30 percent went up from 10.4 million to 12.7 million in the 1990s.

High-Poverty Tracts

In 2000, America's metropolitan areas had a total of 50,502 census tracts and a population of 223 million. The central cities of the 100 largest metros accounted for 28 percent of those tracts (14,060) and 24 percent of that population (54 million), and for 60 percent of the metropolitan poor people who lived in high-poverty tracts in 2000. The number of central city high-poverty tracts increased from 2,595 in 1980 (poor population of 3.4 million) to 3,366 in 1990, and then declined to 3,231 in 2000 (poor population of 4.0 million). The central city dominance in this regard has diminished, however. Their share of the high-poverty tracts in all metros decreased from 67 percent in 1980 to 62 percent in 1990 and stayed at that level in 2000. . . .

In contrast, the suburbs of the 100 largest metros have experienced the most rapid growth in concentrated poverty. There are 23,974 tracts in these suburbs, but only 408 of them were in the high-poverty category in 1980 (482,000 poor residents). Over the next two decades, the number of such tracts grew by 89 percent (to 772) and the number of poor residents grew by 121 percent (to 1.07 million). Their share of total high-poverty area tracts in all metros had increased from 11 to 13 percent in the 1980s and to 15 percent in 2000.

In 1980, 853 of the 12,468 tracts in the other 230 metropolitan areas were in the high-poverty category (with 1.0 million poor residents). By 2000, the number of such tracts had increased by 43 percent (to 1,221) and the number of poor residents by 58 percent (to 1.6 million). However, their share of all metropolitan high-poverty tracts remained relatively flat over this period, increasing from 22 to 25 percent in the 1980s and then dropping back to 23 percent in 2000.

Even though the absolute numbers in the suburbs and other metros went up over the two decades, all saw declines in concentrated poverty *rates* (share of the poor in high-poverty areas) in the 1990s. From 1990 to 2000, those rates dropped from 48 to 41 percent in the central cities of the 100 largest metros, from 12 to 11 percent in their suburbs, and from 29 to 25 percent in the other metros.

Racial Aspects

Changes in the composition of concentrated poverty by race were more dramatic. . . . In 1980, African Americans were the predominant race (more than 60 percent of total population) in almost half (48 percent) of all high-poverty tracts, and those tracts accounted for more than half (54 percent) of the poor population in high-poverty neighborhoods. By 2000, the predominantly black share of tracts had dropped to 39 percent of the poor population in such tracts and to only one-third of the total.

The share of all high-poverty tracts that were predominantly white also decreased (from 18 percent in 1980 to 14 percent in 2000). Compensating increases occurred in the shares that were predominantly Hispanic (up from 13 to 20 percent) and the share that had no predominant race (growing from 21 to 26 percent).

Changes in Population

The way concentrated poverty changes is generally not well understood. Contrary to what the name might imply, levels of concentrated poverty are not much influenced by population growth or decline in tracts that were in the high- or extreme-poverty categories at the beginning of a decade. Rather, the outcome is determined more by the number of tracts moving in and out of those categories. And it is important to know that when tracts reach high-poverty status, further deterioration is not at all inevitable. In fact, even when concentrated poverty was increasing overall many tracts experienced reductions in poverty rates and moved out of the category. The overall increase occurred only because, on balance, more moved in. . . .

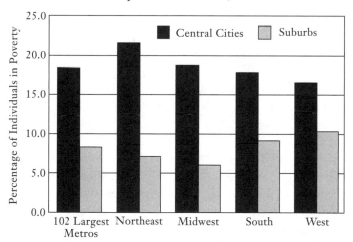

Poverty Rates for Central Cities and Suburbs, 2000

Metro Areas with Population over 500,000

Alan Berube and William H. Frey, "A Decade of Mixed Blessings," August 2002, www.brookings.edu.

In all metropolitan areas, there were 4.9 million poor people living in these high-poverty tracts in 1980. Over the decade, the population of the tracts that stayed in the category (the constant tracts) experienced a net growth of only 151,000. In contrast, the gain from tracts that moved into the category (poverty rates having moved above 30 percent over the decade) was 2.7 million. These gains were partially offset by the loss of 608,000 poor people in tracts who moved out (poverty rates declined to below 30 percent). The addition of new tracts to the high-poverty category clearly had the most important impact in increasing the total to 7.1 million in 1990.

The pattern was quite different in the 1990s. The poor populations of the tracts that stayed in the category experienced a net decline (378,000), and the gain from new tracts entering the category (1.5 million) was more than offset by the loss of tracts whose poverty rates had dropped (1.6 million). The net effect was to reduce the total to 6.7 million by 2000. The gain from tracts entering the high-poverty category in the 1990s (22 percent of the 1990 total) was much smaller proportionally than the comparable gain in the 1980s (55 percent of the 1980 total). . . .

The Demographics of Poverty

Whether the concentration of poverty increased or decreased would not make much difference if there were no corresponding change in indicators of the well-being of the residents of the neighborhoods in question. Census data show, however, that as poverty became less concentrated in the 1990s, there was a change. Conditions did improve in the tracts that were in the high-poverty category at the start of the decade.

Between 1990 and 2000, on average for these high-poverty neighborhoods in all U.S. metropolitan areas,
- the share of people age 25 and over without a high school degree dropped from 48 to 43 percent,
- the share of people age 25 and over who had graduated from college went up from 9 to 11 percent,
- the share of families with children headed by women dropped from 53 to 49 percent,

• the share of women age 16 and over who were employed went up from 40 to 42 percent, and

• the share of households receiving public assistance was cut in half from 24 to 12 percent.

There were some important variations across the country in these conditions and how they changed. . . . The share of adults in high-poverty tracts without a high school degree, for example, ranged from 33 percent (Largely White metros in the Midwest and West) to 54 percent (Melting Pot metros in the West). Improvements occurred in the 1990s in every category on the table, but they were not uniform. The smallest declines occurred in the West (–0.7 percent overall) and then in Melting Pot metros to the Northeast and South (all areas with large and rapidly growing immigrant populations). The largest declines (–9.0 to –9.3 percent) were in the Melting Pot metros of the Midwest and all categories except the Melting Pot metros in the South. . . .

An Astonishing Story

Against the overwhelmingly negative mindset that long dominated America's thinking about cities, our story is astonishing. No writer of a decade ago even hinted at so dramatic a reversal in the concentration of poverty by the end of the [twentieth] century. And it is not just the spatial pattern that changed. By a sizeable number of indicators, there have been measurable improvements in conditions in high-poverty neighborhoods since 1990.

Why did it happen? More research will be needed to answer that in a fully satisfying way. However, it is hard to believe that the booming economy of the late 1990s did not have a great deal to do with it. [Paul A.] Jargowsky's 1997 analysis showed the strength of the local economy as the most important factor in explaining the variation in concentrated poverty across regions in 1990. Contrary to the view that a "culture of poverty" would prevent the residents of the ghettos from ever moving up the economic ladder, his models suggested that if the economy improved, they would benefit. It looks like he was right. Appropriately enough, researchers have been stressing other supports (e.g., the Earned Income Tax Credit, more funding for child care) important to improving outcomes in the late 1990s as well, but a sound economy was fundamental.

While this news is good, two other points should be kept in mind. First while things got better in high-poverty neighborhoods in the 1990s, in most places they got only a little better. In 2000, conditions remained significantly more problematic in high-poverty areas than other neighborhoods with respect to every indicator. For example, those living in high-poverty areas at the end of the decade were still 3.4 times more likely to be receiving public assistance, 2.3 times more likely to lack a high school degree, and 2.6 times more likely to be unemployed than metropolitan residents on average. There is still a long way to go.

Second, there is nothing to suggest that this shift in trends is at all permanent. It is important to remember that the reference date of the recent decennial census (April 2000) was near the peak of the economic boom of the late 1990s. Circumstances most probably have deteriorated again since then, although no one knows reliably by how much.

Nonetheless, the fact that the improvements of the 1990s could occur is important in itself. There are good reasons to suspect that one of the reasons the drive to revitalize America's cities had foundered was that too many people came to believe it was all hopeless, that nothing one could do would make a difference. The 1990s proved that supposition wrong. The story told most often in the past (that things keep getting worse and worse) motivated sympathy, but not action. The story of the 1990s suggests that renewed investment in urban America can pay off.

"Urban crime and the inability of the criminal justice system to deal with it is a continuing focus of public attention in the United States."

Urban Crime Is a Serious Problem

Kevin Early

In the following viewpoint Kevin Early contends that crime is more likely to occur in America's urban areas than in its suburbs or rural towns. Early contends that poverty, unemployment, and drug use have contributed to the problem. He concludes that strategies to reduce urban violence have thus far failed to affect Americans' fear of crime. Early is an associate professor of sociology at the University of Michigan at Dearborn.

As you read, consider the following questions:
1. According to an FBI Uniform Crime Report, what is the rate of serious crime in urban areas?
2. What mechanisms have led to an increase in urban homicide, according to Early?
3. As stated by the author, what is the only crime that is more likely to occur in rural areas?

The recorded data do clearly indicate that rates of violent crime known to the police are higher in urban areas and suburban areas than in rural areas. Urban residents showed higher victimization rates than suburban residents, who, in turn, had rates higher than rural residents. There was, however, relatively little difference in the rape/sexual assault and aggravated assault victimization rates of suburban and rural residents. . . . The 1997 FBI UCR [Uniform Crime Report] indicated that the rates of serious crime were 29.2 per thousand population in rural areas, 36.3 per thousand in the suburbs, and 51.2 per thousand in urban areas. As with violent crimes, property crimes known to the police are higher in urban and suburban areas than in rural areas. . . .

A Disproportionate Problem

Although street crime still is higher in cities than in suburban or rural areas, data from the 1997 UCR indicated that the homicide rate has been on a steady decline for the last five years and that it was decreasing more rapidly in cities than in other areas. . . . The Department of Justice attributed these improvements to better law enforcement.

Most experts conclude that the available data support the notion that "true" rate of crime is probably directly related to the degree of urbanization. After observing that crime rates rise consistently with city size, [Marvin E.] Wolfgang has suggested that the regularity and consistency of the data lead to the conclusion that "criminogenic" forces were probably greater in the city than in less urbanized areas. [J. John] Palen has concluded that even with the serious biases and problems of obtaining reliable crime data, the national problem of crime is clearly an urban problem to a disproportionate degree. [Noel] Gist and [Sylvia] Fava also conclude that even after allowing generously for inadequacies of incomplete data, the differences in crime rates between rural areas or small towns and the larger metropolitan areas are quite impressive.

However, not all observers are equally convinced that the actual rate of crime is clearly greater in the city than elsewhere. For example, [Paul] Horton and [Gerald] Leslie make the following qualifications:

Cities show higher crime rates than rural areas, but it is probable that rural crime is less fully reported. The city also attracts people intending to commit crimes, as it provides more opportunities for crime and provides greater anonymity for those seeking an unconventional mode of life. But there is no evidence that country-reared persons are conspicuously less criminal than their city-reared compatriots.

Different Crimes in Different Neighborhoods

A large body of research exists on the variation in crime rates within metropolitan areas. The basic assumption that the extent and kinds of crime will differ markedly from one part of the community to another tends to be generally supported by this research. One of the earliest studies was that of [Clifford] Shaw, who was among the first to report that delinquency rates decline from the central business district to the outlying areas of the city. He also found that the same pattern held for adult crime, and that rates of recidivism were also highest in the inner zones of the city and declined toward the peripheral areas. Shaw's original study was confined to the city of Chicago, but in a later comparative study of twenty-one cities in the United States and Canada, Shaw and [Henry D.] McKay confirmed that reported crime and delinquency rates were similarly higher in inner zones and slums. [Bernard] Lander found similar results for Baltimore, as did [Calvin] Schmidt for Seattle. Although Schmidt's more detailed analysis found that the central business district, skid row, and contiguous areas had the highest crime rates, it also concluded that each of these areas produced different kinds of crime. The central business district, for example, was characterized by high rates of shoplifting, check fraud, residential burglary (this is possible only in cities having a large residential population in the central business district, as was the case in Seattle), automobile theft, and attempted suicide. On the other hand, the skid row areas were characterized by high rates of fighting, robbery, nonresidential burglary, and disorderly conduct.

In searching for explanations for the spatial patterning of crime, a number of experts have argued that the important factor is not the location or distance from the central business district but rather the social and physical characteristics of the areas in which the crime occurs, or, equally important, in which the offender resides (offenders do not always confine their illegal activities to the areas in which they live). From this perspective, such variables as poverty, unemployment, poor housing, family status, anomie, social rank, ethnic composition, and degree of urbanization have been associated in one degree or another with the incidence of crime. However, there is little agreement among studies such as these as to which of the many variables they identify best explain the tendency for higher recorded rates of crime to occur near the center of the metropolis.

The Effects of Drugs and Juveniles

Throughout the 1980s and early 1990s, drugs appeared to be associated with crime in most major cities across the nation. Increasing violence (i.e., robberies, burglaries, and felonious assaults among juveniles) led to increases in the crime rate. From 1985 to 1992, the rate of homicides committed by young people, the number of homicides committed with guns, and the arrest rate of nonwhite juveniles for drug offenses all doubled (UCR, 1997). Although many of the national trends have remained relatively stable, there has been some dramatic change in violent crime committed by young people. A resurgence of juvenile and adult gang activity in several major cities contributed to increases in homicides and other violent crimes. The mechanisms responsible for high homicide rates included the availability and use of handguns, gang wars, and drug trafficking. According to the UCR, the rates of violent crime in most of the nation's cities began to climb in the late 1960s. The prevalent theory is that many urban centers, abandoned by white populations after racial unrest and urban riots unsettled the nation's cities, declined economically, politically, and socially. A substantial proportion of the increasing incidence of crime was attributable to urban neighborhoods where unemployment, transient populations, and physical deterioration were commonplace. As a result of "white flight," many inner cities are increasingly black or Hispanic. These communities are characterized by poverty, economic dependency, family instability, and high rates of crime.

The crime index rate is highest in metropolitan areas where there have been increases in violent crime (i.e., homicide, assault, forcible rape, and robbery). Suburban and rural areas also reported significant increases in violent crimes. Despite an increase in suburban violence in recent years, crimes of violence continue to be higher in the metropolitan centers than in the suburbs or rural areas.

Although more pervasive in urban America, violent crime is also growing in rural communities. Regardless of offense, urban crime rates are generally higher than rural crimes rates. The only exception occurs in the burglary category where the rural crime rate has surpassed the urban crime rate. Where most Americans live, all crimes except auto thefts have decreased since 1980.

A Growing Fear of Crime

Urban crime and the inability of the criminal justice system to deal with it is a continuing focus of public attention in the United States. Since the early 1960s, Americans have focused on crime and violence in general. Violence is in our homes, neighborhoods, schools, and places of employment. Americans have reported increasingly fearful attitudes toward crime. Despite the prevalence of data showing a decrease in violent crimes, there is a growing public demand for a more punitive criminal justice system. For the most part, public and private responses to urban crime in U.S. society have been relatively reactive. These approaches are often riddled with emotional and political biases that deny the real dimensions of the crime problem.

Attitudes toward drugs and rising public awareness of the relationship between drugs and crime during the 1970s and 1980s has led to national strategies for reducing and controlling urban crime and violence. The strategy reflected a coordinated plan involving the criminal justice system and a collection of education, workplace, and public awareness institutions/organizations. This approach has had limited impact on the nation's perception and fear of crime despite political rhetoric about getting tough on crime, locking up offenders and "throwing away the key."

"The formula for massive crime reduction developed in major cities across America over the past ten years has been tested, and found effective."

Urban Crime Is Decreasing

George L. Kelling and Ronald Corbett

In the following viewpoint George L. Kelling and Ronald Corbett assert that crime in American cities is declining and provide suggestions as to how urban areas can continue to prevent crime. According to the authors, lowering the rates of urban crime requires cities to target small crimes such as panhandling and public drunkenness, remove illegal weapons and guns from the streets, hold the police accountable for the crime rate, and involve community residents in crime-fighting efforts. They contend that those efforts have been responsible for decreasing crime rates in urban America. Kelling is a professor of criminal justice at Rutgers University in New Jersey, and Corbett is the executive director of the Supreme Judicial Court of Massachusetts.

As you read, consider the following questions:
1. What should be "the guiding vision of law enforcement," in the authors' opinion?
2. According to Kelling and Corbett, how does "broken windows" policing reduce the number of criminals in the general population?
3. As explained by the authors, how did the New York City Police Department reduce the problem of drug dealing?

The most impressive achievement of city governance during the urban renewal of the 1990's was the enormous decline in crime. Over the last decade [from 1993 to 2003], police departments across the country adopted innovative new crime prevention strategies and realized unprecedented results. Despite those successes, however, much work remains to be done in reducing crime and increasing public safety. While some cities across the nation have made great strides, driving down the national crime rate to levels unseen since the 1960's, there were many that missed out on the national trend, reducing crime only marginally, if at all. Moreover, from [2002 to 2003], with several notable exceptions, crime rates have plateaued, and in some cities have even begun to track upward once again. If the success of urban America is to continue, it is essential that police departments and civic leaders not rest on their laurels, but rather continue to improve and refine their crime prevention strategies, adopting the most effective methods displayed in recent years.

Two principal goals must guide the creation of strategies to replicate the most impressive crime prevention successes of the 90's: Order maintenance and the creation of law enforcement structures to support it. The guiding vision for law enforcement must be to maintain order within each city, not to catch criminals. Creating an environment that is not conducive to illegality, rather than seeking to punish illegal conduct after the fact, is the key to preventing crime. Having adopted this vision, implementing it on the streets requires that local police units have the resources to do their job properly and the freedom to use them innovatively, and that they be held strictly accountable for the results, whatever they may be. This naturally requires careful tracking of crime patterns and close communication within police departments in order to target resources appropriately and to place responsibility accurately. It also requires the integration of other law enforcement and public sector agencies, as well as the local communities, into an order maintenance framework. By adopting the combination of an order maintenance philosophy and a flexible, accountability-driven law enforcement structure, cities that have made little progress to date can achieve reductions on par with the most dramatic declines in urban crime during the last decade, while those cities that have already experienced such successes can continue to force crime down to ever lower levels.

Proactive Police

The purpose of law enforcement is, ultimately, to prevent crimes rather than to solve them. Solving crimes and punishing criminals is a necessary, but by no means sufficient, aspect of defending the citizenry. In order to effectively reduce crime, law enforcement must focus its efforts on maintaining order within its jurisdiction, eliminating as far as possible the conditions that allow illegality to flourish. To achieve this goal police departments and other law enforcement officials must adopt strategies designed under this vision, rejecting a reactive, after-the-fact, policing approach. They must target factors, such as small-scale public disorder and illegal guns and drugs, that spawn both contempt for the law and ever greater crime trends. They must also work to ameliorate communal problems even before they become criminal, and to employ the advantages afforded by the parole and probation system to exercise control over those people who are statistically most likely to commit crimes. Finally they must manage those problems they cannot solve, accepting that perfect crime prevention is unobtainable and focusing on ensuring that criminal conduct they cannot eliminate has the minimum possible effect on the community.

There is a natural temptation for any police department to focus their efforts on responding to reports of crimes. Certainly it is the least complicated approach. When a crime is reported, the police respond as quickly as possible to stop the crime if it is in progress, or to work the case and catch the perpetrator. Such activities naturally represent a large part of the necessary work of any police force. However, when this kind of response-oriented policing becomes the central mission of law enforcement it will have an extremely damaging impact on the success of crime prevention. Removing criminals from the streets is a means to reducing crime, not an end in and of itself, and police departments cannot afford to focus on it to the exclusion of other, equally important methods of crime prevention. It is crucial, there-

41

fore, that the focus of law enforcement officials be on proactive measures, rather than reactive ones.

Adopt "Broken Windows" Policing

One of those proactive methods, and probably the single most important tool for maintaining order available to law enforcement, is the "Broken Windows" approach to policing. "Broken Windows" policing focuses on small "quality of life" crimes, such as prostitution, public drunkenness and urination, aggressive panhandling, and the like, putting large numbers of cops out on the streets at all times and ensuring that the city's public spaces are free of any illegal activity. When communities fail to enforce laws against these so-called minor offenses, accepting a low level of disorder as inevitable and not worth the trouble of addressing, the result is that the disorder increases and major offenses, from robbery to murder, follow in its wake. Taking action against crime at its most innocuous sends a clear message that illegal behavior will not be tolerated, reducing the incidence of every level of crime.

At the same time, many of those arrested for small crimes prove to be wanted for other more serious offenses. In this way "Broken Windows" policing both reduces the number of current criminals in the general population and creates an environment in which new criminals are far less likely to emerge. The most comprehensive, and successful, application of this policing approach has been in New York City, where a recent analysis of its decline in crime found that between 1989 and 1998 over 60,000 violent crimes were prevented solely by the use of "Broken Windows" policing.

Beyond its effectiveness in reducing crime, this approach to policing is extraordinarily effective in securing many of the subsidiary benefits of a less crime-ridden city. Citizens not only are safer, they feel safer. Robbery of local shops is not merely less likely to occur, storeowners believe they can operate without constant concern. By freeing the streets from low-level disorder as well as high levels of crime, police provide city residents with the freedom from fear that is essential to a flourishing urban environment.

A key principle, intimately linked to "Broken Windows," underlying effective crime prevention is that the proper business of police is problems, not incidents. Response-oriented policing approaches police work as a series of disconnected incidents that had neither history nor future. In fact, most such incidents have both. The factors that lead to a certain crime will usually evidence themselves in one form or another and likely would resurface in similar terms. Thus, incidents of spousal abuse or noisy and boisterous bars, for example, are often indicative of an ongoing communal problem that can be managed or solved before it blossoms into broader illegality. Doing so requires police to engage in activities, from mediating disputes to issuing friendly warnings to loitering teenagers, that do not directly address criminal activity. The tremendous results generated by Boston's "Pulling Levers" program, which explicitly embraced problem solving, provide a perfect example of its effectiveness. Just as adopting "Broken Windows" allows police to stop major crimes by controlling smaller ones, accepting problem solving as a legitimate role and goal for the police can stop bad situations from blossoming into crime.

Targeting Illegal Weapons and Drugs

Illegal weapons are a major factor in exacerbating crime rates. High rates of criminal gun possession tend to increase the overall violence associated with crimes, and are incredibly destructive of public order. It is impossible for a community to believe that crime will not be tolerated if they see people flouting the law by carrying illegal guns on a daily basis, let alone if the night is occasionally punctuated by gunfire. The fewer guns on the streets in malicious hands, the fewer shootings there will be, and the safer and more orderly a city will be.

It is important, therefore, for police to specifically target illegal guns. One strategy simply requires police to check the identification of those stopped for less serious offenses. Persons wanted for other crimes can be searched, and they will often turn out to be carrying illegal guns, which can then be confiscated. This dovetails neatly with "Broken Windows" policing, which naturally increases the number of people stopped for minor offenses. Another effective strategy is to trace how those arrested with illegal guns obtained their weapon. In New York, which pioneered the most aggressive targeting of illegal guns in the 90's, police interrogations of those arrested with illegal guns have netted the arrest of hundreds of gun dealers and record levels of illegal gun confiscations.

Declining Crime Helps the Poor

The sharp decline in crime in America since 1980 has benefited almost everyone by improving personal safety in homes, at school, and on sidewalks, buses, and subways. But the inner-city poor, living in neighborhoods that typically suffered from high rates of violent crime, have by far been helped the most.

The much-improved quality of life in inner cities is the driving force behind the housing boom in downtowns across the country.

Gary S. Becker, *Business Week*, July 17, 2000.

In most cities, there is a clear link between crime and illicit drugs. Crime and drug use follow one another, and where drug markets exist other crime will be practically inevitable. Even more so than in the case of illegal guns, a thriving drug trade engenders contempt for the law, as it is so obviously unenforced. Devoting resources to effective anti-drug initiatives will therefore result not only in reductions in the drug trade, but also make a major impact in reducing other related crimes and restoring order. The central strategy that informs successful initiatives is to blanket areas where the drug trade flourishes and give drug dealers no place to hide. Employing tactics such as "buy and bust" operations, a major uniformed patrol presence, and putting neighborhood drug gangs out of business can transform drug-ridden communities into safe, orderly spaces. Carried out broadly enough, they can have the same effect on entire cities. . . .

Reducing the Impact of Crime

In developing a vision for crime prevention, it is important to recognize that not all crime problems can be solved. Reducing the amount of crime, or even of a particular type of crime, to zero simply isn't a reasonable goal for urban law enforcement authorities. Efforts to reach unachievable targets can sap morale, reduce public confidence, and most importantly lead to a misallocation of police resources. Instead, police must learn to deal with problems without a solution by managing them in a way that reduces their impact on the citizenry to its lowest possible point. For example, prior to the mid-90's, large areas of New York City were infested with drug dealing. Employing a variety of tactics, the NYPD was able to dramatically reduce the problem, but they were, and still are, unable to eliminate drug use and dealing from their city. Realizing this, the police focused their efforts, with immense success, on driving drug dealers off the streets and indoors where, while continuing their illegal activities, they ceased to instill a climate of disorder and lawlessness on the city. Thus, by managing the problem rather than trying fruitlessly to solve it, the NYPD maintained order even where they could not totally eliminate crime.

Applying an order maintenance strategy can only succeed so far without a law enforcement structure that properly supports it. Creating that structure requires extensive central data collection and analysis, and constant feedback and review of the effectiveness of police programs. It also requires the creation of strategic partnerships between the police, other branches of law enforcement such as parole and probation departments and district attorney's offices, non–law enforcement public service agencies, and community groups. Such partnerships are essential both to marshal all the necessary resources government and the public can bring to bear to prevent crime, but also to gain the consent and involvement of each community's members, without which maintaining order within the communities will be nearly impossible. Perhaps most importantly of all, a culture of accountability must be instituted within the structure. At every level, from the whole city to a single street, the law enforcement personnel entrusted with preventing crime must take responsibility for failure, and be recognized for their success.

Police Departments Must Be Accountable

No matter what vision of crime prevention is chosen and what strategies are selected to implement it, no law enforcement organization is likely to succeed in reducing crime unless it is held responsible for doing so. Far too often in the decades preceding the 90's reforms, criminologists and political leaders argued that social, economic, and demographic "root causes" were responsible for crime, and that nothing mere police officers could do would change the crime level afflicting a city. This attitude, which unfortunately still infects a significant portion of the national debate on crime, undermines any attempts at better crime prevention.

Insisting that police don't matter eliminates all the pressure and most of the incentives for them to succeed, saps the morale of officers, and leads inexorably towards a response-oriented brand of policing, the flaws of which were outlined above. A key principle of crime prevention, therefore, must be an absolute insistence on the accountability of police departments for the crime rate. While the police do not have limitless capabilities, and will often require partnerships with other groups to succeed in preventing crime, theirs is the central role. Using the proper strategies, including such partnerships, the police can reduce crime, and failure to do so must not be written off as an inevitable result of amorphous social trends. . . .

Involve the Whole Community

One last crucial component to effective crime prevention is community support. Without the consent, and hopefully active involvement, of the people among whom the police operate, it is extremely difficult to reduce crime. The entire project of maintaining order, after all, is only possible in an area where the majority of citizens actually want order. If the majority opposes the police, denying the consent of the community to their efforts, the community as a whole can itself act to maintain disorder by active opposition to the police. While the extreme version of this phenomenon, such as the Los Angeles riots following the Rodney King case [which involved King's beating by police], is quite rare, even fairly small degrees of community opposition can cripple law enforcement efforts and provide aid and comfort to illegal activity. It is, therefore, absolutely essential to work with leaders in the community being served, and to pay careful attention to the concerns of normal community members.

If gaining community consent is essential, involving community members actively in the effort to maintain order is nearly as significant. Police resources are necessarily finite, and retaking the streets of a neighborhood from disorder and illegality, not to mention keeping them once efforts are directed to other troubled areas, requires the help of the people who live and work there every day. Community residents know what the local problems are and community institutions are the ones that can combat acceptance of criminal activity. Close cooperation with the people crime prevention is designed to benefit must be a part of any law enforcement strategy.

The formula for massive crime reduction developed in major cities across America over the past ten years has been tested, and found effective. Order maintenance–based policing implemented through a law enforcement structure designed to support it has resulted in the most dramatic crime prevention successes in the history of the nation. Continued reductions in crime are certainly possible, even as the national downward trend seems to be coming to a halt. Cities such as New York and Baltimore have seen precipitous crime declines . . . even as crime elsewhere has stabilized or risen. It is not a coincidence that both cities employ an aggressive order-maintenance policing strategy. If other cities wish to continue to see safer streets and more secure citizens, they would do well to follow the same path.

"The inner cities scored a historic breakthrough in the '90s."

The Condition of America's Inner Cities Is Improving

Neal Peirce

In the following viewpoint Neal Peirce asserts that urban America is undergoing a renaissance. According to Peirce, inner cities are improving in areas such as home ownership, income, and job growth. He contends that this economic boom, which began in the 1990s, needs to be supported by people living in the suburbs and by financial institutions in order to continue. Peirce is a journalist and syndicated columnist whose work focuses on America's metropolises.

As you read, consider the following questions:

1. By what percentage did inner-city poverty drop during the 1990s, according to Peirce?
2. How did public housing change during the 1990s, as explained by the author?
3. In Peirce's view, why is it important to revitalize inner cities?

Has the broadly proclaimed renaissance of America's inner cities, launched in the 1990s and continuing into this decade, been real? Have the ghettoes, barrios and other economically lagging areas of our cities made a true and lasting comeback?

Finally there's solid evidence, based on Census tract analysis, to show what's been happening. The data, compiled by Harvard Business School professor Michael Porter's Initiative for a Competitive Inner City, was released at a first Inner City Economic Forum [in New York City in fall 2003].

On the plus side, superstar inner-city areas, including those of Boston, Oakland, San Diego, San Francisco and San Jose, not only gained jobs between 1995 and 2001, but did so faster than their host cities. Inner-city Milwaukee and Pittsburgh even added jobs as their overall cities shed workers.

Yet other inner cities, including Toledo, Rochester, Buffalo, St. Louis and Raleigh lost jobs. Detroit lost a discouraging fifth of its inner city jobs in just six years.

Positive Signs for Inner Cities

On several measures, the inner cities actually outpaced U.S. averages. Median incomes in the inner cities rose 20 percent to $35,000 a year, compared with a national median gain of just 14 percent. Inner-city poverty dropped by 4 percent while average household income grew 20 percent, both outpacing the nation. Percentage gains in housing units and homeownership also exceeded the nation's.

Inner cities did lag in some areas. Their job growth was just 1 percent from 1995 to 2001, compared with 2 percent nationally. With an 82 percent minority population, their total homeownership still trails the nation—32 percent vs. 60 percent. Inner cities have suffered a bit worse than the nation in the recent recession.

But for most of these areas' 21 million people, the 1990s brought an exciting reversal of decades of abandonment and grueling poverty. Inner cities gained economic momentum in tourism, entertainment, finance and services. Major retailers, recognizing big untapped markets, started to return. Assertive enforcement of federal anti-red-lining laws, plus the vision of savvy development firms, sparked major hous-

49

ing and commercial developments.

The inner cities scored a historic breakthrough in the '90s, former Housing and Urban Development Secretary Henry Cisneros told the conferees in New York, as the massive readjustments that they'd faced since the '60s—millions of manufacturing jobs lost, cataclysmic population change, social disruption—finally leveled off.

Dallas's Resurgence

Urban America experienced a renaissance in the 1990s. As it often has, Dallas led the way. While the statistics show that Dallas' population, like that of many central cities, increased robustly over the past decade, the statistics do not paint a full picture of the many exciting things happening in Dallas.

In 1990, downtown Dallas was written off as dead, with no immediate hopes for future revitalization. Today, the resident population of downtown Dallas and nearby neighborhoods has increased dramatically, while the West End, the home of the new American Airlines Center, has become a vibrant urban entertainment district. Downtown Dallas is again competitive with its suburban counterparts.

Ron Kirk, speech before the U.S. Conference of Mayors, April 2001.

And the climate of the decade was right. Cisneros ticked off the factors, starting with the longest economic expansion period of U.S. history, crime reduction led by mayors like New York's Rudolph Giuliani, welfare reform, and a serious start to recycling urban brownfields.

Community development corporations and community finance institutions expanded rapidly. Major financial institutions, from the Bank of America to selected pension funds, started taking a keen interest. And dramatic improvement came to many neighborhoods as public housing units that had once been havens of crime and destitution started to become mixed-income developments under the federal Hope VI legislation that Cisneros helped launch.

But what comes next? What's the formula, asked Porter, "to get market forces to bring inner cities up" to the cities and metro areas that surround them?

A big part of the answer, said Belden Daniels of Economic Innovation International, can be found in a new generation of market-rate, equity-based inner-city investment funds, backed by major banks, insurance firms, foundations and public pension funds. Pioneer funds in Massachusetts, Los Angeles, the San Francisco Bay Area, San Diego and St. Louis have already pumped [money] into inner city businesses, mixed-income housing and other ventures, realizing solid rates of year-by-year returns.

"Now we're up to $2.5 billion of private equity capital in these second generation funds," says Daniels. He agrees this is far from sufficient, given the decades of underinvestment across America's inner cities. "My goal," he asserts, "is that 12 years from now we'll have multiplied this field 100 times to $250 billion, generating $1 trillion in economic activity and matching investors' market expectations."

The Inner Cities Matter to All of Us

Yet on the ground, the going is still tough. Former President [Bill] Clinton dropped by to talk about the merits of targeted, "micro-economic" development where capacity's lacking. With [consulting firm] Booz Allen Hamilton and New York University's Stern School of Business, Clinton has been working with a dozen Harlem companies—and discovering that 80 percent of small businesses in the area operate on month-to-month leases, "totally at the mercy of markets."

Does the fate of inner cities matter to everyone—even affluent suburbanites? Yes, famed Harvard urbanologist William Julius Wilson told the conferees. The higher the ratio of inner city income to suburban income, he noted, the stronger the economy of the entire metro region. "In the global economy, firms choose regions. The health of the inner city is a key factor in their decisions."

Bottom line: Speeded-up inner city revitalization doesn't just deliver healing of a wounded society. It also spells a sounder economic future for everyone.

"The poor are much more likely to live and work in conditions that are detrimental to health."

The Urban Poor Suffer from Serious Health Problems

David Hilfiker

In the following viewpoint David Hilfiker contends that poor urban Americans suffer disproportionately from asthma, anemia, and other illnesses. According to Hilfiker these health problems are exacerbated by a lack of access to affordable health care. Inner-city children are especially vulnerable, Hilfiker argues, because untreated infections and diseases can have long-term effects. Hilfiker is a doctor and author whose books include *Urban Injustice: How Ghettos Happen*.

As you read, consider the following questions:
1. How does poor prenatal care affect children, according to the author?
2. What percentage of Hilfiker's young patients suffers from anemia?
3. According to Hilfiker, why are poor patients with acute ear infections more likely to experience hearing loss?

According to the United States Census, in 2000 over 38 million Americans (14 percent) did not have health insurance *at any time* during the entire year. We tend to assume that if people are poor enough, they are eligible for some kind of governmental health coverage. That assumption is wrong. Less than one-third of the people living in poverty are even *eligible* for Medicaid, the primary form of health insurance available to the poor, and the rate of uninsurance among the poor is over twice as high as among the general population. The low-paying jobs available to poor people rarely offer health insurance coverage as a benefit. It is, of course, out of the question for poor people to purchase health insurance on their own. Even modestly comprehensive family policies currently cost more than $650 a month, half the *total* income of a family of three living at the poverty level, so they remain largely uninsured. This means that in any sort of health emergency the poor must spend a significant percentage of their income on clinic or emergency room visits, especially when young children are involved.

Complicated and Costly

Even those who do qualify for Medicaid must undergo an application process that can be arduous and discouraging. Until the 1996 passage of the legislation known as Welfare Reform, most poor families who received what we usually think of as welfare (Aid to Families with Dependent Children, or AFDC) received Medicaid automatically. Because more than half of these families have been moved off the rolls, they must apply separately for Medicaid, a process that can, in some states, prove virtually impossible for a person who must go to work each day to complete.

Once covered by Medicaid, the poor face a sometimes-insurmountable hurdle: finding a doctor who will accept Medicaid payment. Although patterns vary from state to state, fewer and fewer doctors or hospitals accept Medicaid—largely because reimbursement is usually low—so those who are poor must usually go to hospital emergency rooms or public clinics for their care. But hospitals are not good places to receive routine health care, although they generally handle emergencies well, even for the poor. In fact, federal law requires that any hospital admit and care for emergency patients regardless of ability to pay, but it is now an unusual hospital that offers indigent patients much in the way of continuing care, preventive medicine, or help with routine medical problems. Patients with such problems are increasingly triaged out of emergency rooms. Public clinics can be excellent sources of health care for the patients they accept, but they rarely have the staff or other resources to provide care, much less follow-up, to all who need it. Waits are often long, a different doctor may be seen each time, and there is often no special provision for paying for other needed services like x-rays, lab work, or hospitalization, which can be enormously expensive. And even public hospitals and clinics often try to recoup whatever charges they can from poor clients. So although hospitals may not follow up with aggressive collection routines, patients receive bills anyway.

Thus cost prevents appropriate health care, leading to both poorer health and further poverty. The relationships between health and poverty, however, are complex, for each affects the other. The health of poor people is measurably worse than average: infant mortality, the single most commonly used indicator of population health, is 60 percent greater (and the death rate for newborns is twice as high) for families with incomes below the poverty level than for those above it. Many forms of cancer are more common among the poor. Individuals earning less than $9,000 annually have death rates three to seven times higher (depending on race and gender) than those earning $25,000 or more per year. Poor prenatal care or maternal malnutrition can each lead to learning disabilities and decreased cognitive abilities in children, which in turn can contribute to poor educational achievement, further complicating the experience of poverty.

We know intuitively that poverty can lead to poor health, but research over the last decade has documented that even economic inequality has a separate association with poor health. Studies comparing countries with similar standards of living, for instance, have found that in those with greater levels of economic inequality the health of the entire population (not just the poor) is worse. Similar studies comparing different states in the United States have come up with the same results. The size of the gap between rich and poor matters as well. According to the World Health Organization, the United States, despite its status as the richest country in the world, ranks thirty-second among all nations in the "equality of child survival," a measurement of the distribution of health among different populations within a country. The United States ranks twenty-fourth in life expectancy, and thirty-second in infant mortality, the two most common measures of the health of a population. Over the last twenty-five years, as inequality in our country has increased, we have dropped even further in the rankings. Not only poverty, but also inequality decimates the health of our people.

The Health Problems of Urban Children

Examples of poor health among the poor are everywhere: congenital disease and infant AIDS are far more common among the poor, as are the chronic diseases of childhood. Lead poisoning, asthma, malnutrition, anemia, and chronic middle ear infections are not only expensive to diagnose and treat, but can also lead to permanent impairment. Poor children are twice as likely as affluent children to suffer lead poisoning, for instance, and the long-term, deleterious effects on the brain of lead deposits are well known. Severely poisoned children may suffer seizures, coma, and mental retardation, but even those with milder degrees of lead poisoning are at risk for learning and behavior problems. Language acquisition can be delayed, hyperactivity may result, motor coordination may be affected, aggressive or impulsive behavior is more common, and children may have generalized difficulty learning. In addition to being severe problems in their own right, all these symptoms lead to difficulties in school. These difficulties are compounded when the schools in the poor areas lack the capacity to give the individual attention needed; these children may do poorly or drop out altogether. Lead poisoning means that a child enters the challenge of adulthood in the ghetto even less prepared than peers to cope with it.

Childhood asthma has increased dramatically over the last thirty years. Both poverty and inner-city residence are independent risk factors for asthma, and poor African-American children are more than twice as likely to get asthma as other non-poor children and more than four times as likely to be hospitalized. The death rate from asthma is four times higher among African Americans than among whites. Asthma is not only a serious, potentially life-threatening illness in itself, but among chronic health conditions it causes the most school absences. It is the second leading cause of hospitalization for children aged five to nine and may account for a third of all emergency room visits. For the uninsured, the several medications often combined to treat asthma are prohibitively expensive. Asthma becomes highly disruptive to the life of the child and his or her family, adding further chaos to their lives.

Health Problems Never End

The cycle of poverty can be viewed as both a cause and an effect of ill health, since each tends to perpetuate the other. The cycle of poverty also means that when a child is born into a low socioeconomic status, he or she is not very likely to rise above it. Just as significant, the child's parents and grandparents probably never enjoyed a higher socioeconomic status, either.

The correlation between income and illness is consistent. Patterns of thinking about health and taking care of the body are ingrained into the way generations of low-income people take care of themselves and their families. Disproportional sicknesses don't stop at asthma and lead poisoning. As the former children of ill health grow up, they become adults with serious health concerns.

Maggie Adams, "The Health of the City," Center for Urban and Regional Policy, www.curp.neu.edu.

While measuring "hunger" is necessarily subjective, the United States Department of Agriculture's annual survey of hunger reports that approximately ten million U.S. households, (accounting for 18 percent of the children) are "food insecure" at some point during the year, meaning that they do not have access to enough food to meet their basic needs. Over three million of these households experience hunger at some point during the year. On any given night, 562,000 American children go to bed hungry. Compared to other low-income children whose families do not experience food shortages, hungry children suffer from over twice as many individual health problems—unwanted weight loss, fatigue, headaches, irritability, inability to concentrate, and frequent colds.

Iron deficiency anemia is also a common result. In the middle-class rural community where I practiced for seven years, anemia was rare. I was shocked, upon moving to the inner city, to discover that well over a third of my young inner-city patients were anemic. Average hemoglobin levels (measuring anemia) were significantly lower than my rural patients'. All of the symptoms of hunger, especially when exacerbated by anemia, mean that hungry children are less able to cope with the difficulties of their environment. School performance suffers, with the expected consequences on future earning power.

The Vicious Cycle of Health and Poverty

Sometimes these health problems exacerbate poverty in surprising ways. Consider middle-ear infections (*otitis media*). Normal acute ear infections cause pain and lead to emergency doctor visits, where they can usually be treated easily. Sometimes, however, *acute* otitis media leads to *chronic* otitis media that may have few symptoms and be detectable only by medical examination. If, as often happens among the poor, the acute, painful episodes are insufficiently monitored through follow-up visits, the chronic otitis media may go undetected. For financial reasons, for instance, a poor child is less likely to revisit the doctor after her acute ear infection seems to have gotten better, so the chronic form remains undiagnosed. This chronic otitis can cause a temporary loss of hearing, which may persist through early childhood. Undiagnosed hearing loss often leads to poor school performance, and so to permanent educational deficiencies, making it that much harder to escape poverty as an adult.

Every illness, of course, makes it more difficult to cope with one's environment, so the poor health status of poor children becomes a permanent impairment. The surround of force seems inescapable.

In addition, the poor are much more likely to live and work

in conditions that are detrimental to health. A friend of mine, for instance, cannot afford to move out of her damp basement apartment although the mold spores it breeds severely aggravate her daughter's asthma.

Finally, the stress of simply being poor has been documented to be a real health risk.

The poor get it coming and going.

"Neglect of the plight of America's cities needlessly inhibits U.S. economic growth."

American Cities Are Experiencing Financial Problems

Max B. Sawicky

Federal and state policies have led to budget problems in American cities, Max B. Sawicky argues in the following viewpoint. He contends that security measures instituted in the wake of the September 11, 2001, terrorist attacks have been a burden for municipalities. Sawicky also declares that reductions in aid from federal and state governments make it more difficult for urban governments to provide basic services. Sawicky is an economist for the Economic Policy Institute, an organization whose mission is to promote a fair and prosperous economy.

As you read, consider the following questions:
1. How much money have cities spent on additional security expenditures since the September 11, 2001, terrorist attacks, according to Sawicky?
2. According to the author, what percentage of local government general revenue comes from federal and state governments?
3. What does the author believe should replace Temporary Assistance for Needy Families (TANF) block grants?

The budgets of local governments have been hit hard by both the economy's downturn in the third quarter of 2001 and the costs of extraordinary security measures in the wake of [the terrorist attacks of September 11, 2001]. Inadequate fiscal backup from federal and state governments is resulting in needless disruption of basic public services and ill-advised deferral of capital expenditures. Even though gross domestic product began to grow at the end of [2001], the effects of the third-quarter slump will linger in state and local government budgets. To date, federal and state governments have worsened the plight of U.S. cities by reducing aid and implementing tax cuts that trigger revenue losses for local governments.

Widespread Budget Shortfalls

As early as July 2001 a majority of cities, particularly the larger ones, expected to be in worse financial shape in 2002. Factors cited included rising costs of employee health benefits, public safety needs, and capital spending. In October, driven by new public safety concerns and declines in revenues from sales tax, tourism, and state aid, a majority of cities needed to draw down reserves.

The added security concerns in the aftermath of September 11 didn't help these already strained local budgets. As of February 2002, the National League of Cities (2002) estimated that added security expenditures had cost municipalities an additional $2 billion since September 11. An important component has been overtime pay for police and fire fighters, with some city governments reponsible for protecting airports and water supplies.

Numerous cities are projecting budget shortfalls for what remains of FY [fiscal year] 2002 and are expecting gaps for FY2003. And though major metropolitan areas are particularly burdened, the problems afflict cities of all sizes, in all parts of the country. Cities have responded by instituting hiring freezes, dipping into reserve funds, and raising local taxes and fees.

In Atlanta, Georgia, an $82 million budget shortfall led the mayor to reduce her own salary and personal staff, as well as raise property taxes. The city of Detroit, Michigan, was faced with a $94 million deficit for FY2003 due to revenue reductions and overtime costs for police and fire fighters. Chatham County, North Carolina, was looking at deficits for FY2002 and FY2003; it is dealing with them by instituting a hiring freeze and postponing capital expenditures. New York City faces a projected deficit of $6 billion for FY2003 that it has yet to resolve. [The table in this viewpoint] reports the actual and projected budget shortfalls faced by a variety of U.S. metropolitan areas in 2002 and 2003. . . .

Revenue Sources Are Disappearing

Many current indicators suggest that revenue growth for state and local governments will be extremely weak. A major revenue source—the individual income tax—decreased in absolute terms. Corporate profit tax proceeds are also expected to fall. Federal corporate income tax revenues have decreased in every quarter since the third quarter of 2000.

Cities depend on federal and state revenues, so when aid proves inadequate, the implications are serious. In 1998, over 39% of local government general revenue came from federal and state governments.

The modest increase of $8 billion in federal grants-in-aid expected in the first quarter of 2002 is not sufficient to revive the state-local sector. The National Governors Association reports that state governments faced an aggregate budget shortfall of about $50 billion for FY2002, which for most states ends in the summer. The National Conference of State Legislatures (2002) expects that, in light of shrinking revenue projections, there will be further problems for states in devising budgets for FY2003.

Neglect and fiscal restraint at the federal and state level translates to reduced state government aid and the creation of budget shortfalls at the local level. After FY2002 budgets were passed, most states reduced aid to local governments as part of their across-the-board cuts. In fact, seven states targeted their cuts on aid to local governments. Some states will reduce aid because their aid program depends on a fixed share of a statewide revenue source. The drop in Michigan sales tax proceeds, for example, will mean an automatic reduction in aid to local governments. In California, the Vehicle Licence Fee funds designated for local governments could be tapped by the state to fix its own projected budget shortfall.

Direct federal aid to local governments is also stagnating. One of the most important federal programs to cities—the Community Development Block Grant (CDBG)—is cut by 46% in the Bush budget compared to FY2002. CDBG serves over 1,000 communities and is a key program that provides fiscal flexibility to local officials.

Ignored by the Federal Government

State governments typically resort to cuts in aid to local governments as partial solutions to their own fiscal problems. Such cuts might be fueled by cuts in state taxes or simply by erosion of tax revenues. Insofar as such problems are remedied by cuts in aid, the result will be higher local taxes or cuts in local spending. Typically a state's economy is better

| Budget Shortfalls in U.S. City Governments

(Dollars in millions except where otherwise indicated)

	Population	Budget shortfall Actual FY2002	Projected FY2003	Budget shortfall Actual FY2002	Projected FY2003 (as percent of budget)
New York, NY	7,428,162		6000	0.0%	14.6%
Los Angeles, CA	3,633,591		250		5.2%
Chicago, IL	2,799,050	80		1.7%	
Houston, TX	1,845,967		16		1.1%
Philadelphia, PA	1,417,601		16.7		0.5%
San Diego, CA	1,238,974	15.6			
San Antonio, TX	1,147,213	18		1.3%	
Detroit, MI	965,084	75	94	2.9%	3.7%
San Francisco, CA	746,777		130		2.5%
Baltimore, MD	632,681	8		0.5%	
Boston, MA	555,249		100		5.6%
Seattle, WA	537,150		50		8.0%

U.S. Dept. of Commerce, U.S. Census Bureau, and author's analysis.

served by absorbing such costs at the state level. Local tax increases or spending cuts tend to be concentrated where the economy is weakest.

State governments are often tempted to reduce taxes in the face of a recession. The benefits of such a move are likely to be lacking for three reasons: state economies are porous, which means the benefits of a tax cut spill out of the state; service cuts tend to offset the benefits of a tax cut, since business firms rely on public services to function; and excessive instability in a state's tax code or its service provision are not conducive to a healthy economy.

A particularly serious problem for the states is the growth of Medicaid costs. Growth rates for FY2001 and 2002 exceeded 10%, well above the pace of all other state expenditures and revenues. Costs have grown due to rising caseloads and increasing prices for prescription drugs. Proposals for a change in the federal formula that would alleviate the states' expenses have failed to pass Congress thus far.

The rising Medicaid caseload suggests that welfare reform has failed to improve the ability of low-income families to finance their own health insurance. The reduction in the national welfare caseload has slowed to a crawl. In fact, the fourth quarter of 2001 saw the number of families on the welfare caseload actually increase by a tiny margin of 498 families. The urban concentration of the welfare caseload is well-known. Some cities, notably New York and San Francisco, share in responsibility for financing Temporary Assistance for Needy Families (TANF) and Medicaid.

The likelihood that some states will face heavier burdens than others in financing TANF points to the need to replace the block grant approach with a formula that is sensitive to such local conditions as poverty, unemployment, and state fiscal capacity, among other factors.

The low levels of aid proposed in President [George W.] Bush's budget won't help states much, further suggesting the need for general fiscal assistance to state and governments. For instance, the President proposed a 26% cut in aid for law enforcement. And Congress is notorious for increasing spending in other areas and reducing federal taxes. These federal tax cuts automatically reduce revenues in the states, since state and local income taxes and estate and gift taxes are often "piggy backed" onto the federal system. Repeal of the Federal Estate and Gift Tax in the 2001 tax cut, for instance, is projected to reduce annual state government revenues by $9 billion.

While the Congress has moved to provide some aid to state and local governments, there has been no serious assessment of national needs. The adequacy of present efforts is at least an open question. The actual mechanism for distributing new funds to local governments has yet to be established.

Congress has enacted some emergency aid programs, but the bulk of the funds go to state governments. An example of pending legislation is the President's proposal of $3.5 billion to "first responders" (police, fire fighters, and emergency medical technicians), which goes primarily to states, not to the local governments that employ most of these personnel. By contrast, knowledge of potential security vulnerabilities, and the responsibility to react immediately, is partly vested in local government. There is little rationale for filtering all federal aid through state capitals, as the U.S. Conference of Mayors has pointed out.

Federal policies also affect funding for security measures in our transportation systems. There is new money for the airline industry, on top of questionable levels of bailout funds to the industry, but a gaping silence with respect to rail, sea, highway, and mass transit systems. This seems like a particularly strange oversight when considering that the World Trade Center, after all, was built by the Port Authority of New York and New Jersey, a governing body for regional, land-based transportation systems.

What Cities Need to Do

What the nation's cities need right now is more focus on the following policy remedies:

- The federal government should provide general fiscal assistance to state and local governments;
- The Medicaid formula should be adjusted to ease the cost burden on grantees;
- The TANF grant should be made sensitive to business cycle downturns, poverty, and state fiscal capacity;

- Federal tax cuts that reduce state and local tax revenues should be rolled back;
- More aid for homeland security should flow directly to local governments;
- State governments should not resort to tax cuts for purposes of economic stimulation;
- State governments should not balance their budgets on the backs of local governments by passing along the costs of tax cuts through reduced aid.

Neglect of the plight of America's cities needlessly inhibits U.S. economic growth, disrupts the provision of basic services, and weakens the common defense against terrorist threats to civilian public safety.

Periodical Bibliography

The following articles have been selected to supplement the diverse views presented in this chapter.

America	"More Homeless, More Hungry," January 30, 1999.
American City & County	"The Fat and the Hungry," January 2004.
Awake!	"Cities—Why in Crisis?" April 8, 2001.
Gary S. Becker	"Tough Justice Is Saving Our Inner Cities," *Business Week*, July 17, 2000.
RiShawn Biddle	"L.A.'s Hidden Money," *Los Angeles Business Journal*, December 15, 2003.
Gill Donovan	"Mayors Find Hunger Increasing in Their Cities," *National Catholic Reporter*, December 28, 2001.
Nick Gillespie	"Cincinnati's Bigger Problem—and Ours," ReasonOnline.com, April 20, 2001.
Robert V. Hess	"Helping People off the Streets," *USA Today Magazine*, January 2000.
Paul A. Jargowsky	"Concentration of Poverty Declines in the 1990s," *Poverty & Race*, July/August 2003.
Eli Lehrer	"Crime-Fighting and Urban Renewal," *Public Interest*, Fall 2000.
Myron Magnet	"More Humbug on Homelessness," *Soundings*, Winter 2000.
Anna Quindlen	"A New Kind of Poverty," *Newsweek*, December 2003.
Time	"Cracking Down on the Homeless," December 20, 1999.

CHAPTER 2

What Government Programs Would Improve Urban America?

Chapter Preface

In 1996 Congress passed a law that significantly restructured America's welfare system. Named the Personal Responsibility and Work Opportunity Reconciliation Act, the bill emphasized the transition from welfare to work and reduced the benefits of welfare recipients who did not meet work requirements. The urban poor were particularly affected by the law. As the nation's largest urban community, New York City's experience with welfare reform is worth examining when evaluating whether these measures have helped urban America.

Numerous analysts contend that welfare reform has improved the lives of New York City's poor. In a *New York Post* article, June O'Neill, the director of the Center for the Study of Business and Government at Baruch College, City University of New York, writes that the poverty rate for single mothers fell from 40 to 32 percent between 1996 and 2001 while their average income increased by 20 percent. O'Neill observes, "The commitment to join the workforce has given single mothers the impetus to gain the skills and experience essential to improving their lives." Jason Turner, who served as the welfare commissioner for the city from 1998 to 2001, asserts that welfare reform has helped pull children out of poverty. According to an article he wrote in May 2003 for the Heritage Foundation, a conservative think tank, the poverty rate of New York City children fell from 42 percent in 1995–1996 to 30 percent in 2000–2001.

Other commentators, however, believe that welfare reform has not been as beneficial as the above statistics may suggest. The Committee on Social Welfare Law issued a report in which it questioned the impact of the 1996 law and the way New York City treats its poor. According to the committee, requests for emergency food aid grew by 36 percent between January 1998 and January 1999, and the city's homeless shelters were filled beyond capacity. The committee also claims that the city agency in charge of welfare reform tries to discourage New York's poor from applying for assistance by withholding or lying about the availability of benefits. In addition, while supporters of welfare reform laud the numbers of urban poor finding work, the committee writes, "A 1999 study found that thirty-six percent of parents were either unable to work or lost their jobs due to lack of quality childcare." Another criticism of the welfare-to-work plan comes from lawyer Jonathan Hafetz. In an article for the *Gotham Gazette*, Hafetz criticizes New York City mayor Michael Bloomberg for trying to eliminate education and training programs that would help welfare recipients find permanent jobs that pay better than the "dead-end workfare assignments" they normally receive.

The debate over the effectiveness of welfare reform in New York City is an example of the controversies that surround government programs designed to help urban America. In this chapter the authors evaluate several government policies targeting cities.

> *"The most severely distressed public housing developments can be replaced with viable mixed-income communities."*

Public Housing Programs Can Improve Urban America

Margery Austin Turner et al.

The U.S. Department of Housing and Urban Development (HUD) is the government agency in charge of public housing projects. In the following viewpoint Margery Austin Turner, G. Thomas Kingsley, Susan J. Popkin, and Martin D. Abravanel evaluate the effectiveness of HUD's HOPE VI program. According to the authors, the program—which demolishes distressed public housing units and replaces them with mixed-income housing—has been beneficial to low-income families living in urban neighborhoods. The authors contend that the program has helped poor families to have better housing and has revitalized urban neighborhoods. Turner is the director of the Urban Institute's Center on Metropolitan Housing and Communities. Kingsley and Popkin are principal research associates at the center, and Abravanel is a senior research associate.

As you read, consider the following questions:
1. What is "one-for-one replacement," as explained by the authors?
2. In the view of the authors, why have some public housing agencies failed to respond to the HOPE VI program?
3. What is the final step recommended by the authors to reduce the public housing project failure rate?

O ver the past decade, HOPE VI has brought new energy and creativity to the public housing program. It has produced some of the most promising innovations in the history of federal efforts to revitalize distressed urban neighborhoods. But it is also responsible for some dismal failures, particularly when it comes to the relocation of vulnerable residents. Today, the [Bush] administration proposes to eliminate HOPE VI, arguing that it has served its purpose, costs too much, and takes too long. But by our estimates, at least 47,000 distressed public housing units remain that are not currently scheduled for demolition and replacement. Clearly, the problem that HOPE VI was created to tackle persists; at their worst, these severely distressed developments endanger the lives of the families and children they house and blight the neighborhoods that surround them.

Five Important Lessons

So, whether HOPE VI is resuscitated or replaced with something new, the need clearly continues for a flexible investment initiative focused on the revitalization of distressed public housing. What have we learned from a decade of HOPE VI about how such an initiative should be structured? The Urban Institute's Center on Metropolitan Housing and Communities has just released two major reviews of research on the HOPE VI experience to date that offer five fundamental lessons for the next generation of public housing revitalization.

Mixed-income housing promises to better serve low-income families and urban neighborhoods. Historically, public housing has clustered large numbers of profoundly poor families in low-income neighborhoods, contributing to the concentration of poverty, economic isolation, and neighborhood decline. HOPE VI has demonstrated that the most severely distressed public housing developments can be replaced with viable mixed-income communities. One of the most compelling arguments for income mixing is that the need to attract higher-income residents creates a powerful market incentive for high-quality management and maintenance, improving the housing reserved for the poorest households. And higher-income residents attract more public and private services to the surrounding neighborhood. However, the same mixed-income model won't necessarily work in every neighborhood and market environment. In some settings, it may be possible to attract middle- and upper-income homebuyers to live alongside public housing residents and other assisted renters. But in others, it may make more sense to focus on housing that serves a diversity of lower-income households, including the working poor.

Many who currently live in distressed public housing need extra help through the relocation and revitalization process. HOPE VI has enabled many families to escape from severely distressed public housing to better housing in safer neighborhoods. Vouchers have proven their value as a tool for providing decent, affordable housing to very low income families. But some of the original residents have fallen through the cracks, in part because housing authorities failed to plan adequately for relocation or to offer sufficient support to residents during the process. Future demolition and replacement plans must offer more support and assistance to families that are relocating, including real help searching for housing in healthy neighborhoods and flexible support in making the transition to the private market. Moreover, some residents of distressed public housing face complex problems and challenges (including elderly people with custody of young children, people struggling with drug and alcohol addiction, and people with mental and physical disabilities), making them very "hard to house." It may not be within the capacity of the local public housing agency to meet all these needs, but neglecting them has serious consequences, both for the displaced individuals and for the larger community. HUD [U.S. Department of Housing and Urban Development] and housing authorities should reach out to other local agencies and nonprofits to help tackle the complex needs of hard-to-house residents.

Public housing revitalization should preserve overall levels of assistance for the neediest families. Prior to HOPE VI, the demolition and replacement of distressed public housing was too often stymied by the "one-for-one replacement" requirement, which mandated construction of a new unit of public housing for every unit demolished. Eliminating this mandate and relying instead on the combination of "hard units" and vouchers has proven effective. Still, questions remain about whether the total number of deeply subsidized replacement units compensates fully for the loss of public housing units, even after accounting for the fact that not all the units demolished under HOPE VI were inhabited—or even habitable. In an era of shrinking resources, communities cannot afford to lose housing subsidies. Moreover, if the administration's current proposals are enacted, vouchers will no longer ensure the same kind of deep, permanent subsidy that they do now.

Mixing Social Classes

Would public housing work better if it included a wider range of groups?

That's the experience of public housing in European countries and the argument of poverty experts like William Julius Wilson. Only when poor people are integrated into the life of the larger community will they develop the social networks, role models, and strategies to build better lives for themselves. Federal laws have historically prevented much mixing. The Housing Act of 1949 set public-housing rents at 20 percent lower than the lowest market rents in the area. The Act also allowed local housing authorities to evict tenants with middle-class incomes to make room for poor people. The effect is to restrict housing to the poor, stigmatize the projects, and undermine support for public involvement in housing provision.

The federal HOPE VI program—which aims to destroy bad housing and disperse public-housing tenants throughout the city—builds on this thinking.

Charles C. Euchner and Stephen J. McGovern, *Urban Policy Reconsidered: Dialogues on the Problems and Prospects of American Cities*, 2003.

Public housing is strengthened by the infusion of private capital. Among the most dramatic accomplishments of HOPE VI has been the investment of private capital in the redevelopment of public housing communities. At the start of the 1990s, few could have anticipated that private developers, lenders, and managers would become such substantial stakeholders, or that federal housing resources could leverage much-needed private capital (along with other public resources) to inner-city revitalization. Ongoing private sector investment will be essential to tackle the remaining backlog of distressed public housing. Moreover, the infusion of private capital creates strong market incentives for effective physical and financial management, potentially improving the long-term viability of public housing. But market forces also bring risk; as the role of private investment in public housing expands, safeguards should be crafted to protect the interests of low-income residents and the viability of their housing.

Public housing agencies [PHAs] must be held accountable for their performance. Some PHAs have responded to the HOPE VI opportunity with remarkable creativity and entrepreneurship, reaching out to new partners in city government, the nonprofit sector, and the business community, and creating high-quality, mixed-income developments that enhance the surrounding community. But some lack the organizational capacity to play these challenging new roles effectively. And HUD itself may have difficulty monitoring and supporting these new and more entrepreneurial activities. HUD needs to get better at offering discretion and flexibility to the strongest performers, while providing a combination of support and sanctions for poor perfomers.

Improving HOPE VI

What next? The research record strongly supports continuing a flexible investment initiative like HOPE VI. But HOPE VI (or a successor) can and should be substantially strengthened based on lessons learned to date. More specifically, how would we change the current HOPE VI approach? First, we would argue that a public housing revitalization initiative should be focused not simply on physical redevelopment, but on the contributions that public housing can make to four broad goals: (1) infusion of private capital to public housing, (2) mixed-income communities and the deconcentration of poverty; (3) revitalization of distressed urban neighborhoods; and (4) supportive housing environments for vulnerable families and individuals. HOPE VI has demonstrated that public housing has the potential to advance each of these goals, and that when it does, the results can be impressive.

At the core, funding for the redevelopment of distressed

public housing projects should encourage local PHAs to make more strategic decisions about the use of public housing assets. A single development may not necessarily advance all four of the goals outlined above. But funding proposals should be required to assess a project's potential strengths and weaknesses, and explain how the redevelopment will move the PHA's portfolio as a whole in the right direction. To illustrate, one development may be particularly well suited to providing a supportive living environmnent for a particularly vulnerable group of families, while another's location may make it a good candidate for mixed-income redevelopment. Consistent with sound asset management principles, the key is doing the right thing in the right place.

Furthermore, the revitalization of distressed public housing developments should not reduce the PHA's overall capacity to serve very low income households in decent housing environments. Some revitalization projects may reduce the number of "hard" units with deep public housing operating subsidies. But if they do, the PHA should be required to present a credible plan for either replacing these units in other locations or providing replacement vouchers that are really usable in the local market environment. In other words, PHAs must demonstrate how—using a combination of public housing, other hard units, and vouchers—they will continue to serve as many or more households in the extremely low-income category.

Setting Performance Goals

Next, HUD should develop clear performance standards in each of the demonstration's four goal areas. These standards should define acceptable performance (what it means to "do no harm") as well as superior performance (what it means to meaningfully advance one of the four goals). And they should focus on programmatic outputs and outcomes, rather than process. These standards would be used not only to evaluate funding proposals but also to monitor and assess performance once funding has been awarded. It may make sense to establish a basic set of performance benchmarks for the effort as a whole, through a consultative process with PHAs and other stakeholders. Then, specific performance goals could be negotiated with each PHA for individually funded projects. PHAs that meet their performance goals should be rewarded with greater discretion and flexibility (but not reduced performance monitoring), while PHAs that fail these performance standards should be promptly sanctioned (but not in ways that hurt residents).

Finally, we recommend a step we think would sharply reduce the project failure rate compared to past performance; namely that the new effort adopt more stringent pre-award requirements with respect to PHAs' planning activities and building the partnerships they need to be successful. PHAs with projects meeting threshold criteria would be invited to submit simple proposals describing a basic revitalization strategy. Those judged to be most promising (according to a simplified evaluation process) would be put on a special list of approved revitalization candidates. Candidates would then develop much more solid plans, including feasibility analyses and partnership arrangements, than has been typical in HOPE VI to date. More complete involvement of residents and city agencies in the planning process would also be required at that stage. Where needed, some candidates would be given modest pre-development grants to help cover the costs of planning and making initial arrangements. These pre-development requirements (and grants) would encourage PHAs to commit real time and energy to establishing local partnerships and fleshing out thoughtful plans, rather than simply paying consultants to write winning grant proposals.

In addition to its lessons for ongoing revitalization efforts, the HOPE VI experience has broader applicability to the public housing program as a whole, highlighting the potential for leveraging and mixed-income communities, the power of vouchers, the critical importance of supportive services and compassionate solutions for the hard-to-house, and the ongoing need for effective performance monitoring and management. Recognizing this should encourage further, serious efforts to assess and build upon what has been learned over the past decade so that the full complement of public housing is even better able to contribute to and serve the nation's communities.

> "*[The Department of Housing and Urban Development's] policies and projects actually undercut the kind of development that would indeed help low-income families.*"

Public Housing Programs Will Not Improve Urban America

Paul A. Cleveland and R. Chris Frohock

Public housing programs are economically wasteful and do not benefit urban residents, Paul A. Cleveland and R. Chris Frohock maintain in the following viewpoint. They contend that the Department of Housing and Urban Development's HOPE VI program, which demolishes existing housing projects and replaces them with mixed-income townhome and apartment complexes, will not reduce crime or spur the inner-city poor to improve their socioeconomic standing. Instead, it will displace public housing residents and lead to a faster deterioration of public housing communities. Cleveland is an associate professor of economics at Birmingham-Southern College in Birmingham, Alabama. At the time this viewpoint was written, Frohock was a student at Birmingham-Southern College.

As you read, consider the following questions:

1. According to Cleveland and Frohock, how much money has the Department of Housing and Urban Development spent since the HOPE VI initiative was adopted?
2. What is the best way for people to improve their socio-economic standing, in the authors' opinion?
3. According to the authors, who does HOPE VI reward?

Paul A. Cleveland and R. Chris Frohock, "HOPE VI: HUD's Program of False Hope," *Religion & Liberty*, vol. 12, September/October 2002. Copyright © 2002 by *Religion & Liberty*. Reproduced by permission.

I demand nothing better, you may be sure, than that you should really have discovered outside of us a benevolent and inexhaustible being, calling itself the state, which has bread for all mouths, work for all hands, capital for all enterprises, credit for all projects, ointment for all wounds, balm for all suffering, advice for all perplexities, solutions for all problems, truth for all minds, distractions for all varieties of boredom, milk for children and wine for old age, which provides for all our needs, foresees all our desires, satisfies all our curiosity, corrects all our errors, amends all our faults, and exempts us all henceforth from the need for foresight, prudence, judgment, sagacity, experience, order, economy, temperance, and industry.

In the paragraph above, [nineteenth-century French economist Frédéric] Bastiat satirically attacked the socialist writers of his day for offering up statist solutions for human problems. Likewise, our continuing duty is to expose the fallacies of such statist solutions wherever they may be found. One such example is in the activity of the U.S. Department of Housing and Urban Development (HUD). This government agency has done much over the years to undermine the economic development of cities. In HOPE VI, HUD has reached a new level of vain conceit in its assertion that it knows best how to promote inner city development.

HOPE Is Harmful

HUD was begun in 1965. Since then, it has steadily deteriorated into a mechanism that allows rent seeking and pork barrel spending to increase at a rampant pace. Though HUD has promoted one doomed project after another, some politicians continue to claim that its activities are necessary to accommodate the housing needs of low-income families or individuals. Such a claim is in reality an ugly ruse, because HUD's policies and projects actually undercut the kind of development that would indeed help low-income families and individuals meet their housing needs. HOPE VI is HUD's latest initiative. The project is also called Housing Opportunities for People Everywhere, the Urban Revitalization Demonstration, or the Urban Revitalization Program. Whatever it is called, HOPE VI will have deleterious effects on those residents of the cities receiving funds under its guidelines. There have been other HOPE initiatives. Earlier programs resulted in the development of numerous housing projects that are now considered failures. For instance, the crime-ridden public housing projects that exist in many large cities had their inception in HUD activity. Yet, the failures of these former HOPE programs have provided the impetus to establish additional HOPE initiatives. HOPE VI became law in 1992 as an effort to remedy the failures of previous HOPE programs and was prompted by the recommendation of the National Committee of Severely Distressed Public Housing (NCSDPH). The NCSDPH suggested by report that the physical deterioration of, lack of community services for, and poor management of government housing warranted some kind of action. Thus, HOPE VI is the progeny of a new vision to [according to HUD] "eradicate severely distressed public housing by the year 2000." Since 1992, HUD has rationed out an average of $500 to $600 million every year to public housing authorities around the country.

Has HUD's financial assistance actually improved the lives of the people who had been living in the government's housing projects? Like most government programs, HUD aims to achieve its goals by doing little more than throwing money at the problem. While some of these funds have gone to grants to renovate existing complexes, a large amount of this money has been spent to demolish older public housing. Plenty of cities are always willing to accept these funds from HUD. From 1996 to 2001, HUD awarded 177 demolition grants to cities in 31 states worth $293.3 million. In Chicago alone, HUD awarded approximately $69 million in order to destroy 10,654 housing units. HOPE VI also provides funding for the construction of new projects to replace the demolished housing. In 2001, HUD spent $492 million on revitalization grants that ultimately pay for the construction of new public housing communities. In total, the agency has spent $4.55 billion dollars on its various projects since the HOPE VI initiative was adopted. In effect, the purpose of the program is to destroy older housing in order to build new townhouse communities. According to HUD, the design of the new public housing projects is the key to preventing the failures of the previous initiatives.

However, tearing down existing public housing projects and replacing them with new townhouses will do little to cure the ills that warranted their demolition.

The False Premise of HOPE VI

Two main flaws inhere in the reasoning of HUD officials and others who support HOPE VI. First, HOPE VI immediately displaces the residents of existing housing units wherever such projects are undertaken. The initial phase of the initiative is to destroy a significant number of existing housing projects. The evicted residents receive no meaningful compensation for this displacement and are relocated to other public housing units or left to their own devices to scrounge for any available private housing. Either way, HOPE VI imposes substantial costs on those families and individuals who are presumably supposed to be helped by HUD's programs.

The larger problem with HOPE VI issues from a false premise. [Former HUD secretary] Andrew Cuomo announced in one of HUD's press releases that HOPE VI's aim is to change "the physical shape of public housing by demolishing severely distressed projects—high rises and barracks-style apartments—and replacing them with garden-style apartments or townhouses that become part of their surrounding communities." Therefore, according to Cuomo, earlier public housing projects became "severely distressed" as a result of their architecture being "high rises" or "barrack-style apartments." Crime, drug abuse, and the lack of economic means confronting public housing residents will not be remedied by the construction of prettier housing projects. Cuomo and other proponents of HOPE VI seem to believe that the social problems attendant to public housing communities can be overcome by building houses that look like those that exist in nicer communities. Such is the naïveté of those who promote statist programs like HOPE VI.

In effect, HOPE VI proponents seem to indicate that the crime, drug abuse, and growing shortage of economic means in public housing would not have occurred if the government had simply adopted the correct architecture for the earlier projects and that correcting this mistake should alleviate those social ills. However, Larry Keating, professor at the Georgia Institute of Technology, has aptly pointed out that "social pathologies do not inure in buildings. Destruction of the physical container does nothing to cure the social ills that may afflict the residents within. . . ." It does not follow that simply altering the shape of public housing will stimulate the alteration of the behaviors and lifestyles of people living inside them. The fundamental social problems in government public housing communities have resulted from human action, changing the floor plan and aesthetics of that housing will do little if anything, to address those social problems.

Mixed-Income Communities Are Not the Answer

To bolster their argument, proponents of HOPE VI also focus on the mixed-income nature of the replacement public housing projects, contending that the social ills that pervade existing projects will be cured by mixing people together from a wide variety of economic classes. Cuomo sums up this argument with eloquent, but empty, rhetoric, stating, "We are transforming public housing projects with problems into new mixed-income communities with promise. We are making public housing a launching pad to opportunity, jobs, and self-sufficiency—instead of a warehouse trapping people in poverty and long-term dependence." The implication of Cuomo's statement is clear: Living next door to someone of better economic means will provide all that is necessary for someone else to realize his or her own economic advancement.

Said another way, HOPE VI proponents assume that the establishment of mixed-income communities will provide the motivation and training for residents of public housing to eventually move up the socio-economic ladder and out of public housing. However, simply integrating people who have few economic opportunities together with those of greater economic means does next to nothing to enhance the options for low-income families and individuals. Most people naturally recognize that the surest means to improve socio-economic standing is the adoption of a lifestyle that stresses the virtues of hard work, prudence, temperance, and saving. The grants of HOPE VI actually undercut a person's incentive to adopt such a lifestyle, because it will provide current residents (who weather the displacement) with improved housing regardless of their personal efforts. Such a program neither discourages vice nor rewards virtue. The current social ills that plague government housing will not be meaningfully addressed by having nicer, more affluent neighbors next door or down the street.

Using HOPE VI Grants

(1) Grants . . . may be used for activities to carry out revitalization programs for severely distressed public housing, including

(A) architectural and engineering work;

(B) redesign, rehabilitation, or reconfiguration of a severely distressed public housing project, including the site on which the project is located;

(C) the demolition, sale, or lease of the site, in whole or in part;

(D) covering the administrative costs of the applicant, which may not exceed such portion of the assistance provided under this section as the Secretary may prescribe;

(E) payment of reasonable legal fees;

(F) providing reasonable moving expenses for residents displaced as a result of the revitalization of the project.

Department of Housing and Urban Development, "HOPE VI Guidance," 2001.

Not only does HOPE VI fail to adequately address the social problems of current government housing residents, it also dismisses the hard work of those who have struggled to survive without government assistance. As James Bovard put the matter, "HOPE is a slap in the face to the working poor and lower middle class who stayed out of public housing. The notion that HUD can give away housing to some people without having any adverse effects on their fellow citizens and neighbors is the ultimate left-liberal pipe dream. . . . In effect, the goal of fixing up the projects works at cross purposes with the goal of encouraging residents to find private housing alternatives."

Simply put, HOPE VI aspires to improve the living conditions for only a small number of low-income families and individuals while ignoring the rest. It sends the message [according to Howard Husock] "that need, rather than achievement, is the way to move up the socio-economic ladder in America."

In addition to belittling the importance of achievement, HOPE VI's distribution of resources on the basis of need before merit also neglects biblical admonitions against misguided endowment of funds. In I Timothy 5:9 [New Revised Standard Version], Paul warns Timothy that only a widow who meets certain qualifications, including "devot[ing] herself to doing good in every way," should be included on the list of those whom the church should support financially. Paul indicates here that the church, to which people provide funds freely, should be conscientious about [disbursing] those funds lightly. The grants in HOPE VI, all of which are generated from taxes that citizens must pay to avoid imprisonment, fund public local housing authorities regardless of the current status of the housing projects these authorities manage. Paul clearly believed that the system in the church would be offended by a handout program based on need alone. HOPE VI implements just such a handout program in American society. Paul's admonition, which should analogously be applied to HOPE VI or any other similar statist program, has been either willfully or carelessly disregarded.

Creating Strife and Deteriorating Communities

Beyond the ostensible message of HOPE VI lurks the harsh reality that the program will displace a large number of current public housing residents. For almost every resident in a new HOPE VI low-income housing unit, a past public housing resident has been evicted. This reality has occurred because the grants received by housing authorities have not been spent to replace public housing at a one-to-one rate. Even when a new replacement unit was substituted for one that has been destroyed, some former residents have been precluded from living in the replacement units, because a large number of these units are intended for wealthier tenants. In a 2001 article on the subject, [*Washington Post* writer Debbi] Wilgoren observed that over the life of the HOPE

VI program 97,000 public housing units had been demolished, while only 61,000 units had been built at a total cost of over $4 billion. Therefore, the program has clearly failed to benefit the large number of low-income families and individuals who have been permanently ousted. The immediate option left for these families and individuals seems to be to pack up and move into another slum. It is hard to see how the HOPE VI program benefited these permanently displaced residents at all.

A result of HOPE VI then is to increase the strife among residents of public housing projects. In addition, this program leads to the more rapid deterioration of other public housing communities, forcing their populations to swell. Local housing authorities appear to have turned their backs on finding a solution for problems that exist in these neighborhoods, because the grants awarded by HUD under HOPE VI often go to demolish the most dilapidated complexes. In essence, HUD's new program rewards the unsuccessful management of existing public housing complexes with funds to build new public housing projects.

In the nineteenth century, waves of immigrants came to America in the hope of building better lives for themselves. Many began their lives in this country living in inner-city slum communities. Most of these people eventually moved out of these slums because the fruits of their labor allowed them to afford better housing. The primary effect of programs like HOPE VI is to ignore Paul's admonition by teaching residents of public housing not to implement this American heritage, but to endorse a statist dream that will never come true.

"The living wage is one of the better known and more successful policies designed to address the difficulties faced by low-wage workers."

Living Wages Will Benefit Urban Workers

Jared Bernstein and Jeff Chapman

Living wage ordinances require employers who are contracted by a city to pay their workers more than the minimum wage. In the following viewpoint Jared Bernstein and Jeff Chapman argue that living wage policies improve the economic status of urban low-wage workers by ensuring that people whose work benefits cities can live above the poverty line. While the authors acknowledge that the living wage movement has not fulfilled all its goals, they assert that the overall success of the ordinances indicates that these laws should be applied to greater numbers of the working poor. Bernstein is a senior economist at the Economic Policy Institute, and Chapman is an economic analyst at the institute.

As you read, consider the following questions:

1. What is the "contract model" of living wage ordinances, as defined by Bernstein and Chapman?
2. According to the authors, why would African American workers benefit from living wage laws?
3. In the opinion of Bernstein and Chapman, what is the paradox of the living wage campaign?

Jared Bernstein and Jeff Chapman, "The Living Wage: A Progressive Movement in Action," *Poverty & Race*, vol. 13, January/February 2004, pp. 1–2, 6–7, 10–11. Copyright © 2004 by *Poverty & Race*. Reproduced by permission.

In these times of dominant conservative politics, it's particularly interesting to reflect on the marked success of a progressive policy, one that directly intervenes in the wage-setting function of the private market. We're talking, of course, about the living-wage movement.

A living-wage ordinance is local legislation—typically at the city or county level—that establishes, for workers covered by the ordinance, a wage floor above that of the prevailing minimum wage. There are some 100 living-wage ordinances in place, plus over 70 ongoing campaigns to pass such measures. No two ordinances are the same; they differ in terms of what type of firms or employers are covered, which workers are covered, and the nature of the coverage.

When the contemporary living-wage movement began in the mid-1990s, the "contract model" dominated. Under these ordinances, private firms under contract with the city to provide a service—cleaning streets, maintaining public areas, etc.—are mandated to pay the wage level specified in the ordinance, typically a few dollars above the minimum wage. Many ordinances allow employers to take a dollar or more off the mandated living wage level if they provide health insurance. As the movement evolved, ordinances began to extend coverage to firms that receive a subsidy from the locality. The idea was that if you're an employer who's benefiting from doing business with the city, then you ought not to be creating poverty-level jobs. The way one organizer put it: "It's our money, and as taxpayers, we'd prefer not to subsidize low-wage employers creating lousy jobs in our city."

Thus, from the perspective of advocates, the movement is seen as a way to accomplish a variety of goals. Foremost, to raise the pay of affected workers. Also, by raising the pay in firms with which the city does business, living wages lower the wage differential between public- and private-sector workers. This then can dampen the motivation of city councils to outsource services provided by public-sector workers, whose jobs are usually of higher quality than the privatized version. Historically, the public sector has been an important source of employment opportunities for African-Americans. Higher rates of unionization and affirmative action laws within government employment have ensured higher wages and better mobility than in the private sector. Living wage ordinances also recoup some of financial assistance cities provide to firms that demand such subsidies, and does so in the form of higher compensation to workers. Finally, many living-wage campaigns involve broad coalitions including labor, religious groups, and low-wage workers themselves, giving rise to the possibility of an economic justice coalition that outlasts the wage campaign.

Examples of Ordinances

Why have living wages appeared on the scene, and why have they been so successful? What impact have they had? What is their relevance for minority populations? To what extent are the goals of the movement being realized?

To begin with, we describe a typical living-wage ordinance, just in case one hasn't yet come to your town. Since one of us lives in Alexandria, [Virginia,] where an active ordinance is in place, let's describe that one. The ordinance applies to all non-construction contracts for over $50,000. Firms that win such contracts with the city must pay their workers no less than $10.89 an hour. This equals the poverty line for a family of four whose breadwinner has full-time, full-year work, plus about $2, the average hourly cost of providing health insurance coverage. The wage is indexed to inflation.

As noted, ordinance frameworks are extremely flexible, allowing living-wage campaigners and city councils to inject their particular preferences into the legislation. One flexible parameter is the contract value beyond which firms have to pay the living wage. In Arlington County [Virginia] contracts for less than $100,000 are exempted; in Cincinnati, the threshold is $20,000. In Boston, the original law stated that direct service contracts with the city must be for over $100,000 (for subcontractors, the limit was $25,000), but advocates later successfully campaigned to lower the direct contractors' cutoff to $25,000. The Oakland [California] law requires coverage for workers on service contracts of at least $25,000 and development assistance of $100,000 or more (the tenants and leaseholders of the subsidy recipient are covered). In Chicago and other cities, nonprofits that contract with the city are exempted; in other cities, they are included, though there often exists a threshold here as well in order to exempt smaller providers.

One relatively new application of the living-wage model is in the university setting. A renowned recent example is Harvard University, where student supporters staged an aggressive campaign on behalf of low-wage workers employed by the University directly or indirectly (through subcontractors). The agreement covers security guards, custodians and dining service workers. Along with the initial pay raises, the agreement includes a "wages and benefits parity policy" requiring that outsourced jobs provide wages and benefits comparable to in-house unionized workers performing the same job.

A recent trend in the movement is to push for laws closer in spirit/coverage to the minimum wage. The only active policies of this type are in Santa Fe and San Francisco, both of which were passed in 2003 and require a minimum wage of $8.50 from many of the cities' employers. New Orleans also passed a citywide minimum wage, but implementation was prohibited by the state's supreme court based on jurisdictional issues.

Reasons Behind the Movement

Pragmatic political concerns often generate compromises regarding coverage. This flexibility avoids the "one size fits all" model of, for example, the federal minimum wage, where regional differences are not taken into account. For example, the San Jose living wage is relatively high compared to other ordinances around the nation, but community organizers there pushed for this level based on the very high cost of housing in the Silicon Valley area and the fact that, due to those costs, many of the covered workers had to travel long distances to get to work. In other cases, workers in certain occupations, such as those who work in the school system (as in Milwaukee) might be seen as particularly deserving by influential parties and thus might be strategically highlighted in the campaign and ultimately in the ordinance.

A further motivation for the living-wage movement lies in the negative economic trends that have beset low-wage workers and the lack of federal response. Prior to the late

1990s, this led to falling living standards as incomes stagnated or fell due to a series of forces—deindustrialization, fewer unions, lower minimum wages, high unemployment—that reduced the quality of jobs available to noncollege educated workers. The tight labor market of the late 1990s reversed these trends for a few years, but as the unemployment rate has crept up over the past couple of years, despite the alleged economic recovery, real wage growth is once again stagnant for all workers. Since African-Americans tend to earn lower wages and rely more heavily on those wages to make ends meet, stagnating wage growth is of particular concern to black workers. They are also more likely to benefit from a living-wage ordinance—16% of the workers directly assisted by the most recent (1996) increase in the federal minimum wage are black, despite making up only 11.3% of the total workforce.

Over the long run, the economy has not provided much of a lift for many earning low wages. At the same time, other than the 1996 minimum wage increase, which brought the federal minimum up to $5.15 in 1997, there has been little to no action regarding policies to raise pre-tax wages (a large increase in the federal Earned Income Tax Credit in 1993 and the addition of various state EITCs have, however, made important contribution to raising incomes in families with low-wage workers). To the contrary, what changes have occurred, such as the passage of international trading agreements in the 1990s and highly regressive tax cuts more recently, can be seen as evidence of a more deregulatory approach to economic policy, changes that tend to further reduce the bargaining power of low-wage workers.

In this environment, the living-wage movement offers local organizers a simple, straightforward policy which they can pursue, one with the demonstrable result of raising wages for some of those workers facing these challenging trends.

The Economic Impact

But have the ordinances delivered? Those who opposed the introduction of living wages argue that instead of helping the least advantaged, the wage mandates will lead employers to lay workers off or firms to avoid seeking contracts in cities with living wages (or, in the case of business subsidies, to avoid locating there). What does the evidence show?

A few years ago, this would have been a very tough question to answer. But since then, there has been a great deal of research evaluating living wage outcomes. . . .

The best way to learn about living wage outcomes is to do a before/after study in a city that has adopted the policy. There are two such studies, one for Los Angeles, the other for Boston. Both find that the ordinance lifted wages of affected workers significantly. Regarding job losses, there is some evidence that employers reduced hiring in response to the mandated wage hike, but a closer look at the Boston study suggests that affected firms tended to use fewer part-time workers and more full-time workers compared to unaffected firms—that is, total hours worked didn't change.

Living Wages Strengthen Local Economies

Numerous studies from around the country (including one authored by a well-known critic of minimum wage increases) show that living wage ordinances provide increased incomes to working poor families without causing deleterious effects on the local economy or public finances. In fact, many of these studies suggest that living wage ordinances can strengthen and add vibrancy to local economies by decreasing poverty and inequality, increasing aggregate demand and local buying power, and providing efficiency gains to employers. In addition, many voices from the business community have voiced support for living wages and their positive effects on economic development.

Association of Community Organizations for Reform Now, "Why a Living Wage?" 2003.

Another useful strand of research is by city administrators called upon to report the impact of the ordinance in their city. These reports have the advantage of reflecting information by people who are "closest to the ground" regarding the implementation and impact of the laws.

The city/county studies are summarized in a review paper by Andrew Elmore of the Legal Aid Society of [New York City,] who tells us that the reports ". . . suggest that localities after implementation of a living wage law tend to experience modest contract price increases for a small proportion of contracts," leading to overall increases in contract costs to the city that were usually less than 1%. He does, however, note a few larger increases in individual contracts due to the ordinances, including a 31% increase in a security contract in Hartford [Connecticut] (the only contract covered there), a 22% increase in a janitorial contract in Warren [Michigan] and increases of 10% in about 5% of the city contracts in Berkeley [California].

How do contractors respond to these increases? According to the same study, they appear to absorb at least some portion (in some cases, all) of the increase, and there was little evidence of any diminution of competitiveness in the bidding process. One Ypsilanti [Michigan] town supervisor found that the cost of the ordinance there was held down by an increase in the numbers of bidders. Her explanation was that "now that the wage standard is equal, the ability to compete is based on factors other than wages, so you've got to be tighter and provide less of a profit margin." Other research reports that affected firms take lower profits as the primary means by which they absorb the wage increase.

While the above relates to service contracts, Elmore also reviews the impact of living-wage ordinances as they affect private sector businesses receiving public subsidies, and here the results are more mixed. He reviews nine cities with subsidy-based living wage ordinances and reports that only one—Oakland—reported a decline in the number and size of economic development projects. However, the Oakland example may reveal an important impact of this dimension of the policy. This is a city with a relatively large proportion of underemployed minorities, and while the attraction of low-wage retailers (think Wal-Mart) is surely a double-edged sword, those jobs might still be viewed by local residents as valuable opportunities. We don't mean to imply that retailers will necessarily respond this way when making location choices. Probably, most won't. But some of these retailers—again, we're thinking of Wal-Mart—will go to great lengths to avoid anything that smacks of local regulation, such as wage mandates or union presence. Whether localities want to pursue such "low-road" employers is an open question—there are obvious reasons to avoid engaging in their bargaining strategy—but living-wage advocates should be aware of the possible trade-off.

Imperfect but Successful

So if wages are up with few of the economic distortions that critics worry about, is it clear that the movement is realizing its goals? Yes and no. Living-wage campaigns have been tremendously successful at passing ordinances, and that of course is a first-order goal of the movement. Along the way, they've created a juggernaut, wherein opponents are hard-pressed to fight back against the logic of the ordinance. Any forecast of where this movement is headed would have to predict continued success.

On the other hand, there is a paradox here: The movement's strength is also a weakness in terms of making a serious dent in working peoples' poverty. The primary reason underlying the favorable results from the impact studies, and thus an explanation of why opponents are often unsuccessful in their crusade against these ordinances, is that coverage is very narrow. By remaining limited in the coverage provided by these ordinances, advocates have been able to convince city officials and, by proxy, taxpayers, that they will accomplish their stated goals of raising the economic fortunes of affected workers without leading to economic distortions in the form of significant layoffs, tax hikes, or reduced competition for contracts.

But the marginal coverage of the policy limits its effectiveness to raise the living standards of more than a few thousand workers per ordinance. While no national total of affected workers (those who have received wage hikes due to the policy) is available and is a quickly moving target, a rough count would unlikely surpass 100,000 and may well be closer to half that level. In a low-wage labor market of roughly 30 million, this gives a sense of the limitations of the movement and the nature of the paradox it faces.

As with any new policy, especially one as diverse as this, important questions remain. First, to what extent can coverage be expanded without generating unacceptable inefficiencies? Taken together, much—not all—of the literature on minimum and living wages suggests that given the indeterminacy of wages and the myriad other factors that determine hiring, quite modest wage increases with broad coverage (as in minimum wage increases) and much less modest increases with very limited coverage (living wages) can be absorbed without significant displacements or distortions. If, in fact, the next stage of the living-wage movement is towards expanding coverage, as in minimum wages for all employees in the city, research will be needed to gauge the impact on the relevant outcomes.

Second, even if coverage remains limited, there is the question of spillovers from the living-wage movement, specifically to the labor movement. There is some evidence that living wages successfully diminish the outsourcing of publicly-provided services (by unionized workers), and such effects should continue to be monitored. But a larger question is the extent to which living-wage campaigns can serve as organizing tools for unions. There's not much evidence that the movement has gained much ground in that regard thus far, but there is almost no systematic research on this important question.

At this point, the living wage is one of the better known and more successful policies designed to address the difficulties faced by low-wage workers in the new economy. And, as we have stressed, unless the landscape changes dramatically, the number of ordinances is only likely to grow, perhaps at an even faster rate. The low levels of coverage constrain the policy's reach, but it is a successful political strategy, and one that's targeted at a deserving group of workers. The next step in the movement should be thinking about ways to take it to scale, increasing coverage and reaching greater numbers of the working poor. At the same time, researchers can monitor the impacts, to see if expanding living wages continue to provide higher living standards to low-wage workers without leading to layoffs or other distortions.

"At best, living wage laws bring about modest benefits at a higher cost to businesses and taxpayers."

Living Wages Will Not Benefit Urban Workers

Carl F. Horowitz

In the following viewpoint Carl F. Horowitz argues that living-wage laws, which require employers contracted by cities to pay their employees salaries above the minimum wage, do not benefit low-wage workers. According to Horowitz, these city employees are more likely to lose their jobs as their employers cut personnel in response to the higher-wage costs. Horowitz also asserts that living-wage laws are largely unnecessary; only 15 percent of minimum-wage workers support a family, and most families with at least one minimum-wage worker have an average income that is close to $40,000 per year. Horowitz is a consultant on labor, welfare reform, and other domestic policy issues and a former housing and urban affairs policy analyst at the Heritage Foundation, a conservative think tank.

As you read, consider the following questions:
1. How many living-wage measures had been enacted by 2002, according to Horowitz?
2. According to a study by David Macpherson, how many jobs would be lost in Florida if the state enacted a living-wage law?
3. In the author's opinion what do living-wage advocates exploit?

The "age of the living wage" has arrived with a vengeance. In less than a decade, a well-organized coalition of community groups, labor unions, political parties, think tanks, and churches has coaxed dozens of local governments across the United States into forcing designated employers to pay workers well above the current federal minimum wage of $5.15 an hour. Living wage jurisdictions include major cities such as New York, Los Angeles, Chicago, and Baltimore plus a large number of smaller cities and suburban counties. Local school boards and institutions of higher learning are participating as well. By the end of 2002 there were 103 living wage measures on the books, enacted mostly by municipal and county general governments, and another 74 campaigns actively under way.

Activists defend living wage laws as protecting vulnerable entry-level workers from poverty. They also argue that such laws improve employee morale and productivity, which in turn improves employers' profits. Local governments, to the extent they pay contractors living wages, deliver better services at lower cost. Residents are more satisfied with the quality of life, and the pathologies associated with poverty are reduced. Only exploitative employers and their political supporters lose. Common sense and human decency therefore require national as well as local action in the face of right-wing scare tactics. The federal minimum wage should be made a "living" wage.

The reality is quite different. At best, living wage laws bring about modest benefits at a higher cost to businesses and taxpayers. There should be little surprise in that. As an elevated version of the minimum wage, the living wage magnifies the former's labor market distortions. If applied to all employers in the United States, the living wage would make it far more difficult for first-time job seekers, especially those coming off welfare, to find work. The economic case for the living wage is difficult to make. Indeed, some three-fourths of economists surveyed by the Washington-based Employment Policies Institute [EPI] said that living wage laws would result in employers looking for more-skilled employees, thus crowding out the people with the least skills—the very people whom living wage laws are intended to benefit. . . .

Living Wages Do Not Help the Poor

Advocates of the living wage argue that it combats poverty, but the evidence does not support that claim.

First, the problem for low-income Americans is really insufficient hours rather than insufficient wages. A Bureau of Labor Statistics [BLS] report revealed that in 2000 only 3.5 percent of all household heads who worked full-time 27 weeks or more over the course of the year fell below the poverty line. By contrast, this figure was 10.2 percent for household heads who worked less than 27 weeks. The BLS study also revealed that only a few more than 20 percent of all household heads with below-poverty-line incomes attributed their condition solely to low earnings. The remaining 80 percent cited unemployment, involuntary part-time employment, or one or both of those factors in combination with low earnings. In addition, the Census Bureau reported that the median income in 1999 for household heads working full-time year-round (50 weeks or more) was $55,619. By contrast, household heads working full-time 27 to 49 weeks had a median income of only $38,868, and for those who worked full-time 26 weeks or less the figure was $26,001. An Employment Policies Institute analysis of 1995 Census Current Population Survey data concluded that only 44 percent of minimum wage employees worked full time.

Second, most of the intended beneficiaries of a minimum wage hike do not come from poor households. EPI's analysis showed that at most, 13.3 percent of minimum wage employees were the sole breadwinners of a below-poverty-line family. And all such families (and many above them in income as well) are eligible for the Earned Income Tax Credit. The EITC, which began in the mid-1970s as a pilot program, now adds well over $30 billion a year to the take-home pay of low- and moderate-income families. The 1997 federal tax reform legislation also created a $500 per child tax credit, which Congress later raised to $600 and most recently to $1,000 in 2003.

Finally, a low-wage family's situation is not likely to be permanent. Family heads who earn the minimum wage are typically no older than 30 years of age. EPI research with Census data revealed that only 2.8 percent of employees older than 30 worked at or below the minimum wage. In fact, the average income of minimum wage employees of all ages increased 30 percent within one year of employment.

Only 3 percent of the nation's workers make the minimum wage or less, a proportion that drops to only 1.5 percent of full-time workers, according to Bureau of Labor Statistics data. Some 85 percent of employees whose wages would be increased by a minimum wage hike from $5.15 to $6.15 an hour live with their parents or another relative, live alone, or have a working spouse. About half of those persons—42 percent—were in the first category. Thus only 1.5 percent of minimum wage workers had to support a family, whether as a single parent or as a single earner in a couple with children.

At the same level, too, an increase in the minimum wage benefits mainly those not living in poverty. David Macpherson of Florida State University looked at the effects of New Jersey's 1992 minimum wage hike from $4.25 to $5.05 an hour. He found that the majority of persons who took minimum wage jobs after the increase were young, single, or well above the federal poverty threshold. The average family with at least one minimum wage worker who benefited had an annual income of nearly $40,000.

Finally, the negative employment effects disproportionately hurt the least-skilled workers. Michigan State's [David] Neumark and Federal Reserve economist William Wascher concluded that an increase in the minimum wage would reduce employment of low-skilled teens, but raise it for higher-skilled teens.

Jobs Would Be Lost

At least a half dozen published studies summarized on the Association for Community Organizations for Reform Now's website (www.acorn.org) have concluded that a living wage would have a favorable local impact. ACORN and other activists can be counted on to refer to those studies in public hearings. Local government officials, understandably, are likely to be persuaded; so much research pointing to high benefits and negligible costs could not be wrong. Or could it?

Those studies demonstrate the viability of the living wage

only by removing it from the context of the entire local workforce. That is, the authors are not in a position to consider what would happen if the living wage were applied to the entire local workforce rather than the limited world of government contracting. Existing living wage ordinances affect roughly only 1 percent of all employers in jurisdictions with such laws. What would happen if all, or nearly all, employers were covered?

Living Wages Do Not Create Jobs

The creation of new jobs is one of the most pressing concerns in an economy beginning to regain energy, and the living-wage movement is a splendid way to avoid adding to the labor force. The free market remains the most efficient mechanism to provide wide opportunity, but the market does not recognize organizations asserting that they are interested only in "social justice"—which is to say, power to determine how others work and live.

Woody West, *Insight on the News*, December 8, 2003.

Florida State University economist David Macpherson has conducted three separate studies for the Employment Policies Institute (website: www.epionline.org), each concluding that a living wage would produce serious negative consequences. Two of Macpherson's studies examined what would happen if Florida and California, respectively, enacted a statewide minimum wage at a "living" level. In Florida's case the wage would be raised to $8.81 an hour, or $10.09 without benefits, levels corresponding to Miami-Dade County's law, enacted in 1999. He concluded that the policy would reduce employment by 131,000 to 222,000 jobs statewide and force employers to pay higher wage costs in the range of $4.9 billion to $8.8 billion. Such a state law would not be equitable, either, because many of the projected wage gains would go to secondary wage earners in above-poverty-level families rather than low-income breadwinners. About a third of the wage gains, in fact, would go to families with incomes above $40,000. A more effective and equitable policy, the author argued, would be to offer employers targeted tax credits for hiring the poor.

Macpherson's analysis of the situation in California yielded a similar set of results. If the state raised its minimum wage to $10.29 an hour—the figure cited in a proposed initiative that never made it to the ballot—the result, Macpherson concluded, would be a loss of nearly 280,000 jobs statewide. The youngest and least-educated workers would be the most affected. California employers would incur wage cost increases of more than $12.5 billion a year. And about 30 percent of the wage gains would go to employees in families with incomes over $40,000. Finally, less than a fourth of the affected workers would be the sole earners in families supporting one or more children.

Macpherson also performed a study on the probable impact of a living wage measure passed by Santa Fe, New Mexico, in February 2002 that would apply to most city workers and contractors. The ordinance would phase in, from July 2003 to July 2007, a hike in the local minimum wage from $5.15 per hour to $10.50 per hour. The increase would apply to for-profit employers with 10 or more workers and nonprofit employers with more than 25 workers. Of the 2,700 employees covered by the law, Macpherson expected 154, or more than 5 percent, to lose their jobs. Employers would incur labor cost increases of $6.6 million. More than 20 percent of wage increases would go to low-wage employees in families with incomes of more than $40,000 a year; fewer than a fourth of beneficiaries would be sole supporters of families with children. Of the workers losing their jobs, some 54 percent would be in families with incomes under $25,000, 66 percent would be Hispanic, and 53 percent would lack a high school diploma.

Money Not Going to the Poor

In 2001 the Santa Monica [California] City Council adopted a living wage ordinance that went further in coverage than any other law enacted previously or since. The law designated a "Coastal Zone"—a 1.5-square-mile commercial area—in which businesses and contractors with more than $5 million in annual revenue must pay a wage of at least $10.50 an hour with benefits and $12.25 an hour otherwise. Not long after, UCLA [University of California, Los Angeles] researchers

Richard Sander, E. Douglass Williams, and Joseph Doherty conducted a study on the probable impact of the ordinance. The authors projected net job losses of at least 1,140 to 1,210 jobs, or about 14 percent of all workers covered by the ordinance. One reason for that dramatic impact is that the measure does not allow tip income to be counted toward a worker's wage; tipped employees, mainly in restaurants, would receive from 42 percent to 46 percent of the transfers mandated by the new law. The report offered this prognosis:

> [S]ome of the large retailers and restaurants covered by the Ordinance will see their profits entirely wiped out by the Ordinance, and several of these will cut operations or close down altogether. Overall, we think that the Ordinance will damage, but will not destroy, the economic viability of the Coastal Zone.

Ironically, the overwhelming share of the beneficiaries would not be poor. Of the $49 million in annual direct and indirect wages and benefits, plus administrative costs, the amount actually received by low-income workers residing in Santa Monica would be less than $400,000. The authors concluded, "We estimate that for every dollar spent under the Ordinance, about 7 cents will go to low-income workers for a targeting ratio of roughly 100:7."

Michigan State University's David Neumark has done the most significant research to date on the impact of the living wage. He analyzed data on more than 20 large- and medium-sized cities across the nation in which living wage laws have been enacted. His econometric analyses controlled for as many variables as possible to determine whether factors other than living wage laws could have affected employment and wage levels among low-wage workers.

He concluded that the living wage does raise the wages of low-wage workers. If a living wage is set at 50 percent above the minimum wage, the average wage for workers in the bottom tenth of the wage distribution increases by 3.5 percent. The living wage at that level would lower the local poverty rate by 1.8 percentage points. But that, he cautioned, was only part of the story. For living wage laws also reduce employment among affected workers. A living wage set at 50 percent above the minimum wage would reduce the employment rate for people in the bottom tenth of predicted wage distribution by 7 percent or 2.8 percentage points. "These disemployment effects," he wrote, "counter the positive effect of living wage laws on the wages of low-wage workers, pointing to the tradeoff between wages and employment that economic theory would predict." The primary beneficiaries of living wage laws, he also concluded, are likely to be public employees' unions. By reducing the incentives for cities to contract out work, those ordinances increase the bargaining power of the unions, indirectly leading to higher wages. . . .

An Exploitative Policy

People who push for a living wage insist that the lowest-paid workers are victims of social injustice rectifiable through aggressive political action. They are wrong. The lowest-paid members of the workforce suffer from a lack of skills. In 1994 the Labor and Commerce Departments issued a joint report warning of a widening underclass of workers unable to compete in a complex marketplace. The report spoke of "a large, growing population for whom illegal activity is more attractive than legitimate work."

Organizations such as ACORN stand ready to exploit the discontent of the poor in recruiting them for political cadres. The larger the cadres, moreover, the easier it is for living wage activists to intimidate and shame political opponents as "enemies of the poor." And what local government official wants to be known as an enemy of the poor? Experience bears that out. When the Chicago City Council voted in 1998 to require for-profit city contractors to pay workers in selected occupations a $7.60 an hour living wage, the measure passed 49 to 0. When the New York City Council in 1996 voted 42 to 5 to override Mayor [Rudy] Giuliani's earlier veto of a living wage bill, even opponents conceded that they faced an uphill climb at best. "This was a battle we could not have won in a million years," said one city official. "Council made it look like we were the rich Republicans from the mayor's office, and they were protecting the little guy."

The living wage campaign is a triumph of confrontation

politics and class resentment. By framing the issue as the poor vs. employers, proponents have convinced many local public officials that their campaign is an overdue and unstoppable juggernaut for social justice. It is time for local elected officials to resist a living wage movement that is likely to harm America's poor in the name of protecting them.

"Every day, the economic benefits of public transportation are felt on personal, regional and national levels."

Public Transportation Programs Benefit Urban Workers

American Public Transportation Association and Public Transportation Partnership for Tomorrow

City governments should invest in public transportation because of its economic benefits, the American Public Transportation Association (APTA) and Public Transportation Partnership for Tomorrow claim in the following viewpoint. According to the organizations, public transportation promotes development, creates jobs, and increases tax revenues. They also assert that public transportation helps urban American households save thousands of dollars each year. The American Public Transportation Association is an international organization that aims to expand and strengthen public transportation. The Public Transportation Partnership for Tomorrow is a coalition of businesses and transit organizations that seeks to increase support for public transportation.

As you read, consider the following questions:

1. According to the authors, what construction occurred as a result of St. Louis's light rail system?
2. The average American household spends what percentage of its income on transportation, as stated by the authors?

The evidence is clear: To maintain a sound and vibrant national economy and to enhance Americans' quality of life, the US must increase its investment in public transportation. Providing a broad and sustainable economic stimulus to local communities, metropolitan regions, states and the nation, public transportation:

- Boosts business revenues and profits
- Creates jobs and expands the labor pool
- Stimulates development and redevelopment
- Expands local and state tax revenues and reduces expenditures required for other essential public services
- Reduces household and business costs and enhances worker and business productivity

Increases Revenues and Sales

An investment in public transportation directly benefits the communities where the transportation improvements are made as well as the economies of entire states.

- In St. Louis, a 25-year modernization and expansion of the public transportation system is expected to bring $2.3 billion in business sales.
- In Chicago, the Metra commuter rail system's 20-year "good repair" strategy could add an additional $4.6 billion to business sales.
- Chance Coach, Inc., in Wichita [Kansas], which has provided American Heritage "Streetcars" to over 100 American cities, has generated $50 million in revenue and contributed over $15 million to the Wichita economy.
- Analyses of system expansion for New York City's Metropolitan Transportation Authority and Chicago's Regional Transportation Authority show nearly equivalent statewide economic benefits in relationship to costs: in excess of 2 to 1 for New York State and 1.8 to 1 for Illinois.

"Every $1 billion invested in the nation's transportation infrastructure supports approximately 47,500 jobs—proving that transportation continues to be an economic engine and job creator." These include durable and non-durable manufacturing jobs, as well as jobs in non-manufacturing industries such as construction, finance, insurance and real estate, retail and wholesale trade, and service.

• At plants in Plattsburgh and Hornell [New York] and Sacramento [California] hundreds of workers assemble orders for rail equipment.

• New York's MTA-LIRR East Side Access project is expected to generate 375,000 jobs and $26 billion in wages.

• New Orleans expects the economic activity generated by its Canal Line to create over 1,661 new jobs.

• Tri-Rail of South Florida expects its five-year public transportation development plan to spawn 6,300 ongoing system-related jobs.

Revitalizing Neighborhoods

In communities and regions across the nation, investment in public transportation promotes vital economic growth and development.

Public transportation-oriented development in congested corridors revitalizes neglected and decayed neighborhoods, frequently serving as a catalyst for new business partnerships between public agencies and private businesses. These partnerships are often community-based, involving minority-owned enterprises seeking to establish new economic roots in distressed neighborhoods and communities.

• In Washington, DC, the new $90 million New York Avenue "in-fill" station on Washington Metro's existing Red Line is being developed through an equal partnership between the federal and DC governments and local business interests. The station will trigger significant new mixed-use development, revitalizing an underdeveloped and underserved part of DC.

• The 35-mile MetroLink light rail system in St. Louis has sparked construction of a $266 million Convention Center Hotel, the $60 million Performing Arts Center and the $5.8 million Jackie Joyner Kersee Sports Complex. Revitalization of the area around MetroLink's downtown Busch Stadium Station includes a $160 million renovation of Cupples Station, a 10-building, 12-acre mixed-use development.

Smaller scale, bus-oriented public transportation investments are also spurring economic redevelopment across the country.

• In Dayton [Ohio] the Wright Stop Plaza occupies a historic building and provides easy access to and transfers between most routes of the Greater Dayton Regional Transit Authority. Housing an assortment of shops, the plaza has become a popular downtown gathering place.

• The first phase of Boston's Silver Line Bus Rapid Transit project opened on July 20, 2002. Since the planning process began, over $450 million has already been invested in commercial and residential development in the corridor.

Spurring Economic Development

Public transportation stations attract and concentrate new development, often in livable and attractive arrangements that encourage public transportation use and reduce reliance on private vehicles.

• The Dallas Area Rapid Transit (DART) light rail starter line has generated over $922 million in development, surpassing the $860 million cost of the project.

• Washington, DC's Metrorail has generated nearly $15

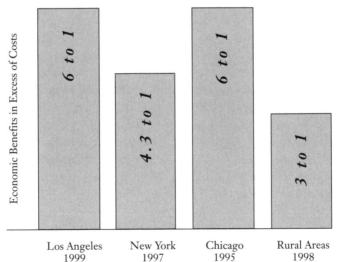

Economic Benefits of Public Transportation Investment

Economic Benefits in Excess of Costs

Los Angeles 1999 — *6 to 1*
New York 1997 — *4.3 to 1*
Chicago 1995 — *6 to 1*
Rural Areas 1998 — *3 to 1*

Cambridge Systematics, Inc., *Public Transportation and the Nation's Economy: A Quantitative Analysis of Public Transportation's Economic Impact*, Washington, DC, October 1999.

billion in surrounding private development. Between 1980 and 1990 alone, 40 percent of the region's retail and office space was built within walking distance of a Metro station.

• Developers in places as diverse as northern Virginia, Portland, San Diego, Denver, Chicago, Baltimore, Los Angeles and New York are investing millions in commercial buildings, sports facilities and entertainment complexes around public transportation stations.

In many areas, traffic congestion is putting the brakes on economic activity. Business leaders stress that increased access results in more commerce and often encourages business and industry to adopt new, more efficient business practices that improve productivity and profitability and reduce costs.

Enhanced and expanded public transportation substantially increases access to and through established business and community centers.

• In Manassas Park, near Washington, DC, the Virginia Railway Express station has jump-started commercial activity, helping revitalize that community.

• The DART system in downtown Dallas sparked a nearly 33 percent jump in retail sales between mid-1997 and mid-1998, as opposed to only a 3 percent rise citywide over the same period.

• In Atlanta and Washington, DC, average office rents near transit stations rose with ridership, and joint development projects added more than three dollars per gross square foot to annual office rents.

The benefits to transportation users of a $10 million capital investment in public transportation will translate into $31 million in added business output and $18 million in added personal income over 20 years.

Benefits to Local and State Governments

Expanded development and economic activity made possible through public transportation help create and sustain the fiscal health of local and state governments and strengthen local economies.

New public transportation-oriented development expands business revenues, leading to new jobs and higher wages and salaries, thus increasing the tax base and revenues flowing to local and state governments. Studies show that, nationwide, residential and commercial property values rise with proximity to rail public transportation systems and stations. Typically, state and local governments realize a 4 percent to 16 percent gain in revenues as a result of increases in business profits and personal income generated by public transportation investment.

• The Washington Metrorail system is expected to generate $2.1 billion in tax revenues for the Commonwealth of Virginia between 1977, when the first station opened in Virginia, and 2010.

• Between 1994 and 1998, the increase in taxable value of properties located near Dallas' DART light tail stations was 25 percent higher than elsewhere in the metropolitan area.

• Riders on Southern Illinois' RIDES program, which serves 11 counties, contribute a combined payroll of over $1 million per year to the rural areas the program serves.

The Personal Benefits of Public Transportation

Every day, the economic benefits of public transportation are felt on personal, regional and national levels. For every dollar earned, the average US household spends 18 cents on transportation, 98 percent of which goes towards buying, maintaining and operating vehicles, the largest source of personal debt after home mortgages. Public transportation can save American households thousands of dollars a year in transportation expenditures.

• Americans living in public transportation-intensive metropolitan areas save $22 billion annually in transportation costs.

• The Altamont Commuter Express, running 77 miles between Sacramento and San Francisco, can cut annual commuting costs in half, from $5,300 to $2,700.

• Fannie Mae's pilot program, which provides "location-efficient" mortgages, recognizes that households' transportation costs are reduced significantly with proximity to transit, enabling families to afford better housing options.

As a fundamental component of our economic safety net for individual Americans, public transportation provides for fuller participation of all Americans in the nation's economy, a wider range of economic opportunities for individuals and businesses, and more avenues for business and industry to increase productivity and reduce costs.

• In Atlanta, BellSouth is consolidating its suburban offices into three downtown locations convenient to the MARTA rail and bus system in order to increase productivity by making commuting easier.

• The location of Motorola's new cellular phone factory at the end of the Metra commuter rail system in Harvard, [Illinois,] greatly expands the labor pool from which the company draws workers.

• In Detroit, the Job Express service operated by the Suburban Mobility Authority for Regional Transportation connects 800 employers and 16,000 jobs.

• Treasure Valley Transit, in Canyon County, ID, provides 91,000 residents spread over 583 square miles with access to jobs, schools and healthcare providers.

• In Wyoming, the Sweetwater Transit Authority helps residents in a 10,000-square-mile area access work sites.

Public transportation provides wide-ranging and lasting economic benefits at the local, state and national levels. To compete successfully in the global economy, our economic strategy in the years ahead must include a solid commitment to increase investment in and use of public transportation.

"It would cost less than $10 billion to provide cars for all the transit riders who don't have access to them."

Public Transportation Programs Do Not Benefit Urban Workers

Wendell Cox

In the following viewpoint Wendell Cox asserts that cars, not public transportation, will improve life for the inner-city poor. He argues that if the government provided cars for people who would otherwise rely on public transportation, it would save the United States billions of dollars and give urban residents access to more jobs. Cox is a senior fellow at the Heartland Institute, a research organization that supports privatization, deregulation, and individual rights.

As you read, consider the following questions:
1. According to data cited by Cox, what percentage of transit riders lack access to a car?
2. What segment of the population does Cox note would not benefit from a "cars for the poor" program?
3. Why does the author believe that moving jobs toward the suburbs would not be problematic?

Wendell Cox, "Why Not Just Buy Them Cars?" www.heartland.org, July 6, 2004. Copyright © 2004 by the Heartland Institute. Reproduced by permission.

A [2004] report from the Federal Reserve Bank of St. Louis confirms what many light rail skeptics have been saying for some time: It would be less costly to buy new cars for transit riders than build and subsidize new rail systems.

The Fed report says it would be considerably cheaper to give a new Toyota Prius to each low-income rider of the St. Louis light rail line, and replace it with a new Prius every five years, than it is to operate that rail line.

Mass Transit Does Not Help the Urban Poor

One of the principal justifications for public aid to transit is to provide mobility to low-income people who cannot afford cars. Federal data indicate approximately 70 percent of transit riders do not have access to a car for their trips.

But transit clearly is incapable of providing much mobility for the poor. For decades, virtually all new urban-area jobs (in the U.S. and throughout much of Europe and Canada) have been established in places that have little or no transit service. For example, a Federal Transit Administration report found there were virtually *no* jobs in the growing suburban Boston employment areas that could be reached conveniently by transit from low-income central city districts.

Mobility is crucial to both affluence and prosperity. A person with a car can get to a job anywhere in a sprawling modern urban area, whether Portland, Phoenix, Perth, or Paris. A person dependent on transit can at best get to downtown or to within a fairly constrained area of the urban core. As for suburb-to-suburb commuting by transit, that takes time—much time—and is often not even possible.

Research by Steven Raphael and Michael Stoll of the University of California–Berkeley indicates nearly one-half of the unemployment rate gap between African-Americans and non-Hispanic whites would be eliminated if virtually all African-American workers (like non-Hispanic white workers) had cars.

Simply stated,

- Transit costs more than travel by car.
- People with cars can get places faster and can go places transit riders cannot.
- Automobile drivers can access more jobs, which means

their potential for getting better jobs is enhanced.
- Where people can travel to more jobs, a community's prosperity is enhanced.

Car-Sharing and Car Ownership

In the U.S., we could provide cars for all travel by low-income transit riders for less than what we currently spend on transit subsidies. It would cost less than $10 billion to provide cars for all the transit riders who don't have access to them, compared with annual spending of about $25 billion on transit subsidies.

A commercial model for such a program already exists. Around the world, anti-automobile activists have established "car-share" networks that allow people to have access to cars without having to own them. For example, "Flex-Car" in Portland provides cars for less than $0.30 per vehicle mile—a rate that includes the car, insurance, service, and fuel.

Transit and Driving, 1990–2000

(Billions of trips or miles)

	1990	2000	% Increase
Transit Trips	8.8	9.4	6.8
Transit Passenger Miles	41.1	47.7	16.1
Urban Vehicle Miles	1,275	1,665	30.6
Rural Vehicle Miles	869	1,085	24.9

American Public Transportation Association and *Highway Statistics 2000*, Table VM-2.

Today, car-sharing is seen as a substitute for car ownership. But its larger market may be to replace public transit systems. Flex-Car's Web site offers packages that allow up to 3,000 miles per month for $700!

Transit riders generally don't travel nearly that much (neither do average automobile drivers, for that matter). But if transit riders were allowed the freedom of a car, they would travel farther. If transit riders were to double their travel, the cost under Flex-Car's volume discount pricing system would be less than $15 billion, still $10 billion less than the annual cost of transit subsidies.

Of course, a "cars for the poor" program would not accommodate all needs. The most obvious need would be for people physically incapable of driving. The U.S. currently spends less than $2 billion on dial-a-ride services for this market segment. Even if those services were doubled, at least $6 billion in transit subsidies would go unused if cars were provided to all low-income transit riders.

The Economic Effects

That leaves the transit riders who own cars yet choose transit, called the "choice" market in the transit industry. They represent at most 30 percent of the transit-riding population. Converting transit subsidies into cars for the poor could mean large fare increases for these remaining riders. Unprofitable services would have to be cut. But why are we subsidizing these people in the first place?

What public purpose is served by a system that forces working poor and moderate-income taxpayers to subsidize high-income executives riding a commuter rail train from Fairfield County to Grand Central Station in New York, or from downtown Chicago to O'Hare International Airport? Why should such executives not pay the full cost of their travel? They do in Tokyo, Osaka, Nagoya, and Hong Kong.

Eliminating transit subsidies could be a problem for downtown areas. In the long run, more jobs would be in the suburbs and fewer downtown. But that's not necessarily bad. The principal jobs-housing imbalance in the modern American or European urban area is that so many jobs are concentrated in a small space in the core, while housing is widely dispersed. If more jobs were dispersed, traffic would be more manageable and less severe.

This is a thought experiment, not an actual proposal for converting transit subsidy programs into automobile options for low-income transit riders. But it demonstrates the extremely high cost, limited success, and unfair distribution of benefits of the current transit subsidy scheme. It is time to start considering alternatives that would provide greater value for taxpayers and more choices for transit riders.

Periodical Bibliography

The following articles have been selected to supplement the diverse views presented in this chapter.

Sharon Hays	"Off the Rolls," *Dissent*, Fall 2003.
Bruce Katz and Katherine Allen	"Cities Matter," *Brookings Review*, Summer 2001.
Michael W. Lynch	"The Hassle Factor," *Reason*, December 2000.
Caleb Mason	"Pedal Revolution," *In These Times*, April 29, 2002.
Charles R. Morris	"The 'Living Wage': It Couldn't Do Any Harm," *Commonweal*, October 11, 2002.
National Catholic Reporter	"Cities That Pay a Living Wage Find It Works," August 16, 2002.
Nation's Cities Weekly	"Intelligent Transportation Systems Help Local Governments," November 27, 2000.
Melvin Oliver	"American Dream?" *Crisis*, September/October 2003.
Chhandasi Pandya	"Affordable Housing in Crisis," *Z Magazine*, November 2003.
Todd S. Purdum	"Mass Transit Riders Are Pawns," *New York Times*, October 29, 2000.
Louis Uchitelle	"By Listening, Three Economists Show Slums Hurt the Poor," *New York Times*, February 18, 2001.
Beverly G. Ward	"Welfare and Transportation," *Witness*, July/August 2002.
Woody West	"Living Wage Can't Compete with Hard Logic," *Insight on the News*, December 8, 2003.

CHAPTER 3

How Can the Lives of Urban Children Be Improved?

Chapter Preface

A frequent conservative criticism of modern American families is that too many are led by single parents. Commentators assert that children who are not raised by both a mother and a father are more likely to live in poverty, struggle academically, and commit crimes, among other serious consequences. Children growing up in urban America are seen as particularly vulnerable; consequently, many analysts argue that marriages should be encouraged among urban families.

One of the leading advocates of urban marriage is Wade Horn, president of the National Fatherhood Initiative. According to Horn, in a column in the *Jewish World Review*, "Children fare much better when raised in a married, intact, two-parent household. In addition, research indicates that both married men and married women are happier, healthier, and wealthier than their unmarried counterparts." He maintains that many unwed urban couples with children are interested in marriage but rarely follow through because society does not do enough to encourage these unions. Horn writes, "How many urban schools teach the skills necessary to sustain a healthy and mutually satisfying marital relationship? The answer, of course, is very few. The consequence of our reticence to talk about marriage, especially in low-income communities, is that young couples aren't encouraged to move towards marriage." Horn further notes that the U.S. tax system makes marriage an economically undesirable decision for lower-income Americans. According to Horn and other analysts, "marriage penalties" prevent lower-income married couples from receiving much-needed welfare benefits.

Another advocate of urban marriage is political scientist James Q. Wilson, who asserts that impoverished urban neighborhoods often lack the stabilizing presence of fathers. In an interview for the public television program *Frontline*, Wilson observes, "There are men present, but they're not fathers. They're mobile impregnators, on the streets, living in gangs, working in crime, selling drugs, going in and out of prison, playing around with alcohol and other women." He argues that marriage is uncommon in these communities because there is no positive model of marriage for young urban adults to emulate.

Not everyone believes that children growing up in American cities need two parents, of course. For example, Trish Wilson writes in the magazine *Feminista!* that these calls for marriage undermine the important role of mothers and seek to establish parental authority. As the debate over marriage in urban settings illustrates, devising effective solutions to the problems urban youths face is challenging. In the following chapter the authors examine some of the suggestions for improving the lives of those young people.

"There is a clear need for more systematic assessments of curfews as a possible tool to combat juvenile delinquency and gang activity."

Curfews Can Be Effective in Reducing Delinquency

Andra J. Bannister, David L. Carter, and Joseph Schafer

While their usefulness has not yet been wholly proven, juvenile curfews can help reduce crime in urban areas, Andra J. Bannister, David L. Carter, and Joseph Schafer assert in the following viewpoint. According to the authors, law enforcement in cities with juvenile curfews claim that such laws reduce vandalism, graffiti, gang activities, and other crimes. Bannister is an assistant professor of criminal justice at Wichita State University in Kansas. Carter is a professor of criminal justice at Michigan State University, and Schafer is an assistant professor at the Center for the Study of Crime, Delinquency, and Correction at Southern Illinois University.

As you read, consider the following questions:
1. According to the authors, during what hours are nighttime curfews most commonly in effect?
2. What is the point of curfews, as indicated by the authors' study?
3. In the opinion of the authors, what are some of the programs that could complement curfew ordinances?

D espite more than one hundred years of use in cities throughout the country, the efficacy and impact of curfews on youth crime remains largely unknown. It has been shown that curfews are correlated with (but do not necessarily cause) lower driver fatality rates among juvenile drivers. . . . In a similar vein the imposition of curfews by parents has been shown to be related to juvenile substance abuse. . . . Although the outcomes of these studies do not support the curfew-crime rate relationship, they do demonstrate that curfews may yield positive effects as observed through some outcome measures. . . .

The purpose of this study was to respond to specific policy inquiries made by police agencies to the authors' community policing centers. Data were collected from a national sample using survey research methods (described below). The instrument was developed to identify and measure expressed factors of interest to police decision makers in a simple, quick format. The variables were based largely upon interviews and comments of police officials with refinements made based on findings of related research. Importantly, the survey items reflected a policy orientation. Once drafted and placed in format, the instrument was pretested on a small purposive sample of police managers (not from the study's population) to assess the survey's clarity, flow, and ease of response. Two additional iterations of the instrument were made before it was ready for mailing.

The study population was defined as all municipal and consolidated police departments serving populations of 15,000 inhabitants or larger in the United States. Using proportional sampling by state, based on Census data, a random sample of 800 agencies was selected using a comprehensive, commercially available directory of law enforcement agencies. After the sample was drawn and the initial mailing had been sent, it was discovered that three agencies no longer existed because each had been consolidated with another police department. Consequently, the actual sample size was 797 agencies. There were 446 usable responses returned representing all fifty states for a response rate of 56 percent. In addition to the survey findings, the authors have interviewed various police officials and conducted site visits to gather further information about the use and effectiveness of juvenile curfews.

Prevalence of Curfews

Survey results found that slightly over two-thirds (67.7 percent) of the responding jurisdictions had juvenile curfews, with 9.6 percent having some form of curfew in effect during the daytime as well as at night. The day curfews were interesting in that they augmented truancy laws and could also be used to investigate young people aged 16 for whom truancy laws did not apply. Some of the day curfews were extraordinarily restrictive. For example, in one city the wording of the daytime curfew ordinance stipulated that if a child was not in the specific place required by law and regulation, the child was in violation of the curfew. This was even applied in the schools—for example, a student who "cut" a class was in violation of the curfew since he/she was not in the place required by school policy (i.e., the student's schedule).

Despite the occasional perception that the use of curfews was on the rise, respondents indicated that their curfews had been in place for a number of years. Among those agencies with juvenile curfews, most (68.9 percent) had been in place for more than five years. Only 3.3 percent had been created within the previous year.

With respect to age, responding jurisdictions seemed to reflect the belief that curfews were necessary or most effective for youth throughout their "juvenile" years. (*n.b.* [*nota bene:* note well] There is some variance between the states in the definition of a juvenile.) More than half (52.7 percent) of the nighttime curfews restricted youth ages 16 or younger while an additional 40.3 percent of the curfews were applied to youth through the age of 17. The remaining seven percent had a wide variety of age parameters, apparently based on local idiosyncrasies and perceived problems. This would seem to support the conclusion that communities view curfews as appropriate restriction on youth throughout their young-adulthood. Those jurisdictions reporting the use of daytime curfews generally indicated they were in effect from 8:00 or 9:00 A.M. until 3:00 P.M. Nighttime curfews were most commonly in effect from 11:00 P.M. until 6:00 A.M. during the week (Sunday through Thursday nights) and from midnight until 6:00 A.M. on the weekends (Friday and Saturday nights).

Jurisdictions which did not have a curfew ordinance were asked to indicate why this was the case. . . . Although there does not appear to be a specific consensus, some of the more common reasons were because political leaders did not want them (63.2 percent) and the police lacked resources for enforcement (50.0 percent). Despite concerns among some legal scholars, the absence of curfew ordinances in responding jurisdictions did not indicate a concern for their constitutionality. Rather, most of the jurisdictions (81.6 percent) had reasons other than constitutionality for not having a curfew.

Jurisdictions not having a curfew were asked if they were likely to adopt an ordinance within the following year. Most of these agencies reported that future adoption was unlikely. In most cases (80.7 percent), agencies indicated that it was unlikely that their city would create a curfew in the next year. Despite the attention curfews have received in recent years, it would appear that their existence is rather stable. Most curfew ordinances have been in place for some time. In addition, most communities not having a curfew do not appear to be interested in their future adoption. Interestingly, comments on the survey indicated that many police departments would like to have a curfew, but did not believe an ordinance would be enacted in their communities.

In most cases (95.6 percent), jurisdictions with curfew ordinances felt that their enforcement was a wise use of police resources. This assertion was made despite the fact that more than half (58.6 percent) of the respondents felt that most juveniles picked up for a curfew violation would recidivate. This is a curious contradiction as one would expect that curfews would only be a wise use of resources if their enforcement was going to prevent future violations. It would seem that police departments perceive some other utility in curfew enforcement beyond preventing the perpetuation of such offenses among juveniles. In this regard, comments suggested that the curfew was a useful tool (i.e., excuse) to stop suspicious young people, notably gang members. In one scenario described to the authors, an officer said that if he saw a "young looking" gang member, that person could be stopped to determine if he/she was in violation of the curfew. Even if the young person was an adult, the stop was "lawful" and anything produced as a result of the stop (e.g., weapons, drugs) would be lawfully seized. One might argue that such practices violate the spirit of curfew laws thus making them unconstitutional or, at least, unethical. . . .

Curfews Are Seen as Effective

Many of the respondents (58.6%) stated that even though a juvenile is picked up for a curfew violation once, he/she will probably violate the curfew again. This does not necessarily erode the perceived utility of curfews as a tool to reduce delinquency and criminality among juveniles. Rather, these responses may reflect the belief that sanctions for violating curfews may not be severe enough to deter future offenses. The point of curfews, it was noted in both the data and comments, was not whether a young person obeyed the curfew ordinance, but whether the curfew had an effect on reducing other crimes for which juveniles are involved. In other words, the police were more concerned with whether the curfew reduced juvenile crime than with whether they obeyed the ordinance.

The data strongly support the belief among the respondents that curfews were an effective tool for reducing various crimes. Most noteworthy was that 93.5% of the respondents agreed that curfews had an effect on reducing vandalism, 89.1% agreed they had reduced graffiti, 85.7% agreed curfews contributed to the reduction of gang activity, 84.7% agreed that curfews reduced rates of nighttime burglary, and 81.1% agreed that curfew enforcement had reduced auto theft. . . . Certainly curfews are not the only factor in these reductions, however, they may hold an important key when such consistencies are observed across various jurisdictions. Moreover, the respondents did not feel the curfews were simply displacing the juveniles to other jurisdictions (60.6%). It must be noted that these responses are based upon the respondent's perceptions, which are not necessarily based on empirical evidence.

The comments in particular noted that the curfew was one element—although frequently a "cornerstone"—in a multifaceted strategy to deal with gangs and youth crime. Intuitively, respondents credit the curfew as a significantly important variable. In all likelihood, however, any effects of the curfew were interactive effects [of] the curfew with other youth-oriented programs. Interestingly, comments indicated that school policies and changes in parental controls over children either did not change or had no effects on youth crime and gangs. Logically, these factors cannot be discounted. The notable aspects of these perceptions is that the police tend to feel that they must shoulder a disproportionate burden of controlling youth crime and misconduct.

Respondents reflected the belief that curfews have utility which goes beyond simply addressing juvenile delinquency and disorder. . . . [As the table in this viewpoint indicates] the vast majority of respondents (90.6%) feel that curfews are an integral part of community policing, most likely as a result of the preventive orientation curfews are intended to achieve. In addition, more than three-quarters (76.3%) of the respondents believed that enforcing a curfew ordinance helped police officers to determine if juveniles were breaking other laws (perhaps by providing officers with the probable cause to stop juveniles). [The table] also reflects the belief among respondents that other community members interested in the welfare and activity of juveniles (specifically, schools and parents) supported aggressive curfew enforcement. Finally, it is interesting to note that many respondents (60.7%) disagreed with the suggestion that curfews displace juveniles into other locales in which there are no curfews.

The Future of Curfews

The findings of this survey provide important insights into the use of, and logic behind, curfews in American communities from the perspective of local law enforcement agencies. The presence of curfew ordinances would appear to be a stable phenomena. Most existing ordinances have been in place for some time, and most jurisdictions without an ordinance indicated that this situation was not likely to change in the near future. Agencies which use curfew ordinances believed that they were effective tools in reducing a wide variety of juvenile crimes. Agencies which did not have an ordinance to enforce indicated that this absence was most commonly due to political forces and agency resources.

Curfews and Police Policy

	Strongly Agree	Agree	Disagree	Strongly Disagree	Don't Know
Curfews are an integral part of community policing. (N=297)	35.7%	54.9%	5.0%	1.0%	3.4%
Parents support aggressive enforcement of curfew laws. (N=292)	11.6%	61.0%	20.5%	2.4%	4.5%
The curfew "displaces" juveniles to go to other locales where there is no curfew. (N=293)	4.4%	27.3%	55.6%	5.1%	7.5%
School officials support aggressive curfew enforcement. (N=297)	23.9%	54.9%	6.7%	0.7%	13.8%
Curfews are used as a tool to determine if juveniles are breaking other laws. (N=296)	17.2%	59.1%	18.2%	2.4%	3.0%

These findings may also help to guide future evaluative research in identifying possible outcome measures by which to assess the efficacy of curfews. It should be noted that although this study focused on crime rates as possible curfew outcomes, there are a variety of other measures which could be employed (i.e., drug and alcohol use, traffic fatalities, citizen perceptions of safety, the degree of severity of juvenile crime, level of gang activity, etc.). The findings also shed light on factors which may motivate police organizations to use (or not use) curfews. As this study has indicated, not every jurisdiction with a curfew chooses to aggressively enforce this ordinance. Consequently, future research efforts need to account for this variable degree of enforcement in determining the efficacy of curfews.

There is a clear need for more systematic assessments of curfews as a possible tool to combat juvenile delinquency and gang activity. Although many police agencies and municipalities have claimed to demonstrate that their curfews have an impact on these outcomes, such conclusions are not necessarily based on systematic evidence. This absence of research is surprising given the enduring legacy curfews have as a method of social control within our country. The true impact of curfews remains unclear and it is uncertain if the prior (dated) research correctly demonstrates that curfews decrease and displace crime.

Perhaps the challenge for the future is to look at ways to decriminalize curfews while still taking actions to show youth that such violations will not be tolerated. Some communities have shown great innovation in pursuing such efforts by designing curfew enforcement programs which do more than just sanction youth who violate the ordinance. If curfew ordinances are designed to "push" youth off the street with the threat of a quasi-legal sanction, many of these other programs are designed to complement them by simultaneously "pulling" in youth. Common elements of these programs include: creating a "curfew center" outside of a central police lock-up where violators may be processed and held for their parents; staffing centers with social service providers; using sanctions beyond fines, including counseling (both individual and family) and community service; offering recreation and job programs; and running anti-drug and anti-gang programs. The effect of these innovations is "to transform the juvenile curfew from a reactive, punitive response to a proactive, intervention against the root causes of juvenile delinquency and victimization" (Office of Juvenile Justice and Delinquency Prevention, 1996: 4).

Future experimentation with curfews would be wise to look at the broader context in which these violations occur. If communities are requiring youth to be off the streets during certain hours, would these efforts be more effective if youth had alternative forms of entertainment? When a violation is detected, is it always appropriate to respond by citing the offender and/or the offender's parents? It is possible that curfews may be more efficacious if communities take steps to create non-punitive sanctions. Programs which offer on-site counseling may allow officials to determine why a youth committed a curfew violation and allow them to intervene when necessary. The key to the future success of curfews may lie in examining programs which provide elements to "pull" youth off of the streets and, in doing so, complement the ordinance's "push."

"Curfews . . . are founded in the 1990s prejudice that all youths are criminals."

Curfews Do Not Reduce Crime by Urban Adolescents

Mike Males

In the following viewpoint Mike Males asserts that cities that institute juvenile curfews do not experience a decline in crime. According to Males, curfews do not work because the vast majority of teenagers are not criminals. He concludes that cities that do not enforce curfews enjoy a greater decline in crime than do cities with curfews, and argues that these laws are unnecessary and make it more difficult for police to target real criminals. Males is a sociologist and the author of several books, including *Kids and Guns: How Politicians, Experts, and the Press Fabricate Fear of Youth*.

As you read, consider the following questions:
1. What are curfews an expression of, in Males's opinion?
2. According to the author, what were the effects of the Vernon curfew?
3. In addition to curfews, what other panaceas have had little effect on crime, according to Males?

Mike Males, *Kids and Guns: How Politicians, Experts, and the Press Fabricate Fear of Youth*. Monroe, ME: Common Courage Press, 2000. Copyright © 2000 by Mike Males. Reproduced by permission.

Hundreds of cities nationwide have instituted and enforced strict curfews on youths being in public at night or during schooldays. Accolades for curfews cascade from politicians and police absent evidence they accomplish anything other than making adults feel better.

The federal government's only document drawn up to support the White House's pre-cast political campaign for both daytime and nighttime curfews was the embarrassing *Curfew: An Answer to Juvenile Delinquency and Victimization?*, by the U.S. Department of Justice's Office of Juvenile Justice and Delinquency Prevention (OJJDP). It declared: "Comprehensive, community-based curfew programs are helping to reduce juvenile delinquency and victimization."

A Misleading Report

The only evidence the report provides is police assertions from six cities designated by OJJDP for having "established comprehensive, community-based curfew programs." The report mixes up crime reported to police with juvenile arrests. It cites only the types of crimes that support its argument. It picks and chooses wildly varying time periods to compare. It includes no follow-up to see if the reported crime declines persisted. It includes no comparisons with cities that did not enforce curfews, the minimum requirement to reach a conclusion as to effect. The report's shoddy quality is suspicious, since OJJDP—with the numbers-stuffed Bureau of Justice Statistics next door—easily could have put together consistent, comprehensive statistics to analyze the issue scientifically.

Examples from the OJJDP report: after three months of enforcement, Dallas, Texas, police reported that "juvenile victimization during curfew hours dropped 17.7% and juvenile arrests declined 14.6%" (why three months, especially since crime displays seasonal variations?). Phoenix police reported "a 10% decrease in juvenile arrests for violent crimes" during the 11 months (why 11 months?) following the curfew's advent. Chicago police reported that juvenile burglaries, vehicle theft, and theft declined (measured by arrests over varying time periods). New Orleans police reported "a 27% reduction in juvenile crime during curfew hours in 1994 compared with 1993" (measured by arrests, a claim later research demolished—see below). Denver police reported that "serious crime dropped 11% during each of the first 2 years of the program" and "motor vehicle theft dropped 17% in 1994 and 23% in 1995" (measured by crimes reported to police). North Little Rock police reported a reduction in violent crimes reported to police of 12% and a burglary decline of 10% from 1991 to 1992. (OJJDP didn't bother to follow up to see if this crime decline persisted; FBI reports show crime was back up again in 1993–95 to levels higher than in 1991.) Jacksonville, Florida, did not report results but was praised anyway.

As will be shown from the Monrovia case examined below, and as sociologist William Chambliss points out in *Power, Politics & Crime* (Westview Press, 1999), police have been known to diddle with statistics to produce desired results. In cities where juvenile arrests went up after curfews took effect, police claimed the increase resulted from more cop contact with youths that uncovered more crime; when juvenile arrests declined, police claimed it reflected a real crime decline. Even assuming all the above police reports are honest, some types of crime will decline in any given community and time period. In fact, crime declined in nearly all cities during the 1990s; what about those cities (including others claiming spectacular crime declines, such as Boston and New York) that did not adopt juvenile curfews?

As one of the few researchers to date to study this question on a comprehensive basis, I think the evidence is overwhelming: curfews are nothing more than an expression of modern adults' unwarranted fears of adolescents, and they probably make the streets less safe. In an exhaustive study with the Justice Policy Institute published in the Winter 1998/99 *Western Criminology Review*, co-author Dan Macallair and I found that whether measured over time, by county, by city, or by specific case study, juvenile curfews had no effect on crime, youth crime, or youth safety.

No Reduction in Crime

Using annual Criminal Justice Statistics Center figures and Department of Finance demographic data for California and its 12 largest counties for 1980 through 1997, we compared periods of high curfew enforcement with reported crime rates, juvenile arrest rates, and juvenile violent death rates. We found no effect. We examined reported crime, juvenile arrests, and juvenile violent death rates logged one year behind years of high curfew enforcement to see if there was a delayed effect. No effect. We analyzed crime rates in all 21 cities of 100,000 population or more in Los Angeles and Orange counties for 1990 through 1997 to see whether crime was reduced in cities with high levels of curfew enforcement. It wasn't. We performed two detailed case studies comparing crime, juvenile arrests, and juvenile violent deaths in cities that had received national attention for strongly enforcing juvenile curfews with similar-sized, nearby cities that did not enforce curfews. If anything, the cities that did not enforce curfews enjoyed better results.

One of our most interesting findings was that after the Los Angeles suburb of Monrovia imposed its famous curfew banning youths from being in public during school hours (heartily endorsed by President [Bill] Clinton and trumpeted as a "success" by a fawning press), police tabulations showed crime declined considerably faster during the hours the curfew was not in effect (the summer, and school-year evenings, weekends, and holidays) than when it was enforced (school hours). Comparing the three years after the curfew's advent in October 1994 with the corresponding periods before, we found that crime dropped 29% during school-day hours when the curfew was in effect—but it fell by an even more impressive 34% during school-year evenings and weekends, and by 43% during summer months, when youths were allowed to be in public! Monrovia police later admitted their initial claims of great curfew benefits, recycled by Clinton and the press, resulted from mathematical errors. These revisions drew no media or White House attention.

At the same time, the Los Angeles Police Department released two studies of curfew enforcement. The first, in February 1998, reported that a spectacularly intense curfew enforcement effort (4,800 curfew citations in one district) "has *not* significantly reduced" juvenile crime or victimization (emphasis original). In fact, these increased compared to districts where there was no curfew enforcement! The second report, issued in July 1998, found that sharply reduced efforts yielded better results.

In the March 2000 *Justice Quarterly*, University of Central Florida and New Orleans criminologists released their large-scale study of New Orleans' curfew, funded by a U.S. Department of Justice grant. The study examined 120,000 victim records and nearly 20,000 juvenile arrest records. It found the curfew, though vigorously enforced with 3,500 arrests and $600,000 in police overtime in the first year, did not reduce crime, juvenile victimizations, or juvenile arrests. Temporary decreases in violent and property victimizations after the curfew took effect evaporated; the "more permanent" effect was an increase in victimizations over time. The conclusion as to why "juvenile curfews are ineffective" was straightforward:

Delinquent behavior does not occur in isolation, but in a social context consisting of an individual's peers, school, and family. . . . These factors are complex and cannot be addressed simply by passing a law requiring youths to be off the streets during particular hours.

Even given these findings, it might seem counter-intuitive that police removal of youths from public wouldn't at least cut thefts, burglaries, and other public crimes during curfewed periods. In a 1999 follow-up study, I got some insight as to why curfews don't work. . . .

Why Curfews Fail

The occasion was a challenge by the Connecticut Civil Liberties Union [CCLU] to the juvenile curfew in Vernon, a suburb of Hartford. After a juvenile was shot to death by an adult during the daytime, the city imposed a nighttime curfew on youths to fight "gangs and drugs." About as logical as most 1990s crime-busting panaceas.

The Vernon curfew took effect in September 1994 and banned youths from being in public between 11 P.M. and 6 A.M. The initial effects were dismal. In its first six months, crime in Vernon was sharply higher than in the corresponding months of 1993–94 before the curfew began. Over the next three years, serious crimes reported to police fell by

11%. This was also not impressive. Vernon's decrease was considerably less than the average crime decline over the same period in the dozen other Connecticut towns of similar size (–14%), the state as a whole (–15%), and 600 similar-sized cities nationwide (–13%). More to the point, crime declined the most rapidly in Connecticut's two cities of similar population that did not enforce curfews, Wallingford (–17%) and Middletown (–24%).

Curfews Are Racially Biased

[An] objection raised to curfews is that they may result in racial bias. Police in several states, most recently New Jersey, have been caught out using a practice known as race "profiling", which targets minority groups—typically for traffic offences. Art Spitzer of the American Civil Liberties Union insists that however good the intentions of the . . . curfew, the actual enforcement will inevitably single out poor, mostly minority, children in inner cities, who usually don't have swimming pools or air conditioning to "go home to."

Economist, September 18, 1999.

Further, the major (Part I) crime that declined the most after Vernon imposed its curfew, aggravated assault, was the one least likely to be committed by juveniles, while crimes more common to youths, such as burglary and robbery, did not decline as much. A simple correlation analysis showed slightly (though not significantly) more Part I crimes in months with more curfew arrests. Finally, crime declined faster in the two years before Vernon imposed the curfew than in the two years after. Add it up: police figures showed no reason to credit Vernon's curfew with cutting crime in general or youth crime in particular. Why didn't it?

As part of the CCLU case, police turned over all 410 individual curfew citations handed to 16- and 17-year-old violators from January 1995 through June 1998. The citations provided a wealth of detail concerning what youths were doing at the time of the stop. The snapshots of the nighttime lives of several hundred Vernon youths constitute an excellent random survey challenging not only the official notion of a generation out of control, but the avalanche of popular books asserting today's teens are a "tribe apart," lost en masse to secret lives of drugs, drinking, crime, and violence.

What were the kids up to when the cops cruised up? The large majority were with friends, walking, sitting on park benches, in cars at the drive-in, walking or driving between friends' houses and home. Police specifically were looking for evidence of juvenile endangerment, crime, and gang activity. They found, in 410 curfew stops, only seven cases evidencing other crimes (two outstanding warrants, one illegal weapon, two auto thefts, and two suspects with burglary tools), plus one runaway. Police reported zero instances of juvenile alcohol or drug intoxication, zero evidence of gang activity, and zero cases of youths being in danger (though several were escaping discord at home). If you stopped 400 adults at random, say, members of congress, you'd find more wrongdoing than that.

What the curfew accomplished, then, was to occupy police time removing law-abiding youths from public places. This left more vacant, less-policed streets that provided more opportunities for the criminally inclined. As a raft of urban experts, including Jane Jacobs and William H. Whyte, point out, public places emptied of average citizens are more dangerous and crime plagued. This may explain why Vernon, Monrovia, and other cities experienced greater crime declines during periods when curfews were not enforced—a pattern affecting larger cities as well.

Curfews, in contrast, are founded in the 1990s prejudice that all youths are criminals and ignore the ability of the majority of teenagers to deter crime. . . .

Pointless Policies

As research accumulated in the late 1990s and 2000, the easy panaceas promoted by President Clinton and police interests began to fall by the wayside. Boot camps for youth offenders accomplished nil, a Youth Today analysis reported. Three Strikes laws, trying juveniles in adult courts, and tough drug-law enforcement stuffed juvenile detention facilities and adult prisons but failed to cut crime, a series of Justice Policy Institute studies reported.

In a March 4, 2000, feature, the *New York Times'* veteran

crime reporter, Fox Butterfield, assessed crime trends in cities around the country. Even though politicians, law enforcement, and crime experts had broken both legs getting to microphones to praise their get-tough policies for the late-1990s crime plunge, Butterfield found that cities around the country had pretty much the same declines in crime, regardless of their police policies—including cities that had no coherent anti-crime policy at all. Also that month, government-funded researchers writing in the staid *Justice Quarterly* seemed startled at how "ineffective, quick-fix, and piecemeal" their study found juvenile curfews such as New Orleans' to be. University of Central Florida criminal justice professor K. Michael Reynolds and University of New Orleans sociologists Ruth Seydlitz and Pamela Jenkins called for more research on "why ineffective laws are popular, the functions served by these laws, and the climate that enables such laws to be enacted."

The 1990s big anti-crime policies did not cut crime; perhaps they were never meant to. After all, emerging prison, drug, and treatment interests profit from more, not fewer, offenders. The politicians whose campaigns they bankroll gain more by sounding tough than by doing good. The damage done by the Clinton presidency's sophisticated promotion of simplistic, absurdly fruitless, sound-bite friendly nostrums is incalculable; the only surety is that his reign represented one of the pointlessly cruelest eight years in American politics. The conservative ideologues of the administration of new [president] George Bush Jr. seem poised to do more damage yet.

"Since the Milwaukee voucher program was established on a larger scale in 1998, it has had a positive impact on public school test scores."

Vouchers Benefit Urban Students

Paul E. Peterson

Voucher programs enable urban youth to receive better educations than they would in their local public schools, Paul E. Peterson asserts in the following viewpoint. According to Peterson, these programs—in which families are given money toward tuition for private schools—have proven beneficial in several American cities. He contends that private schools offer many advantages to urban students, including higher test scores, less violence, and smaller classes. Peterson is the editor in chief of the magazine *Education Next* and a professor of government at Harvard University.

As you read, consider the following questions:
1. During the 2002–2003 school year, how many students in Milwaukee received vouchers, according to the author?
2. According to a study cited by Peterson, what percentage of African American adults favor vouchers?
3. Why does Peterson believe public schools will not suffer if voucher programs are implemented?

For many years, fears that school vouchers were unconstitutional slowed their adoption by many state legislatures. But in 2002, the Supreme Court found in the case of *Zelman v. Simmons-Harris* that the Cleveland school voucher program was constitutional. The Court declared that the program did not violate the Establishment of Religion Clause of the U.S. Constitution, as plaintiffs had argued, because it allowed parents a choice among both religious and secular schools. There was no discrimination either in favor of or against religion. Now that school vouchers have passed this crucial constitutional test, many state legislators and other state officials are giving more thought to the voucher concept. In addition to Cleveland, experiments are underway in Milwaukee, Florida and Colorado and are under active consideration in many other states. This [viewpoint] seeks to answer some of the questions that are frequently raised.

How Vouchers Are Used

Simply defined, a voucher is a coupon for the purchase of a particular good or service. Unlike a ten dollar bill, it cannot be used for any purpose whatsoever. Its use is limited to the terms designated by the voucher. But like a ten dollar bill, vouchers typically offer recipients a choice. For this reason, distant relatives find coupons popular birthday presents for those whose tastes are unknown. The birthday child can be given a toy store coupon, without dictating the exact game or puzzle.

It is not only in the business world that vouchers or coupons are used. Food stamps, housing allowances for the poor and federal grants for needy students are all voucher-like programs that fund services while giving recipients a range of choices. Now, the idea is being advanced as a way of enhancing school choice as well. If parents are given a school voucher, the money will certainly be spent on education. But instead of requiring attendance at the neighborhood school, no matter how deficient, the family is given a choice among public and private schools in its community.

In other words, a school voucher is something like a scholarship to be used at one's choice of school. Indeed, in the United States there are numerous privately funded scholarship programs that operate much like school voucher programs. They allow the parent to pick the private school of their choice, but they pay approximately half the tuition for more than 60,000 students in New York City, Washington, D.C., Dayton, Ohio, and many other cities across the country. Although these private programs have generated valuable information about school vouchers, as discussed later in this [viewpoint] more important are the publicly funded ones enrolling over 25,000 students in Milwaukee, Cleveland and Florida. Colorado's newly enacted voucher program is to begin in the fall of 2004. All of the programs are restricted to low-income or otherwise disadvantaged children.

The oldest program, established in Milwaukee in 1990 at the urging of local black leaders and Gov. Tommy Thompson, was originally restricted to secular private schools and to fewer than 1,000 students. In 1998, the Wisconsin Supreme Court ruled constitutional a much larger program that allowed students to attend religious schools as well. In 2002–03, over 11,000 students, more than 15 percent of the eligible population, were receiving vouchers up to $5,783, making it the country's largest and most firmly established voucher program.

The Cleveland program, enacted in 1996, was of lesser significance until the Supreme Court made it famous. Before the decision ruling it constitutional, vouchers amounted to no more than $2,250 and were limited to approximately 4,000 students. After the Supreme Court decision, the number of students increased to over 5,000 and the amount of the voucher in fall 2003 could go as high as $2,700.

The initial Florida program, established in 1999 after Gov. Jeb Bush had campaigned on the issue, initially had less than 100 students but is poised to become somewhat larger. In this program, vouchers are offered to low-income students attending failing public schools. (The Colorado program, scheduled to go into effect in 2004, has a similar focus.) Initially, only two schools in Pensacola were said to be failing, but in 2002, 10 more joined their ranks. A second Florida program, which offers vouchers to students eligible for special education services, has received less attention but is perhaps more significant. In 2002–03, over 8,000 of

Florida's special education students were enrolled in nearly 500 private schools.

In other words, a variety of privately and publicly funded voucher programs are in operation. Much can be learned from taking a closer look at how they operate in practice.

Benefits to Urban Minorities

Most voucher programs are focused on low-income or otherwise disadvantaged families, because their children are the ones least well served by traditional public schools. Voucher proponents point out that middle-income whites can pick their school by moving into a desired neighborhood or using a private school, while low-income blacks cannot easily do so. As voucher proponents love to point out, school choice is already part and parcel of the American educational system. Every time parents identify a neighborhood to live in, they select a school for their child—often self-consciously. According to a recent survey, 45 percent of whites (as compared with 22 percent of African-Americans) consider "the quality of the public schools" when deciding where to live. Since African-Americans have the least amount of choice among public schools, they benefit the most when choice is expanded.

In evaluations of private voucher programs in New York City, Washington, D.C., and Dayton, Ohio, my colleagues and I found that African-American students, when given a choice of private school, scored significantly higher on standardized tests than comparable students remaining in public school. In New York, where estimates are most precise, African-American students who switched from public to private schools tested, after three years, roughly 8 percentage points higher than African-Americans in public schools— nearly a two grade level improvement. These test score gains were accomplished at religious and other private schools that had much less money than that available to New York's public schools. Data available from the state of New York reveals that New York City's public schools have twice as much money per pupil as Catholic schools do—even after deducting amounts spent on the food lunch program, special education, transportation-related expenditures and the cost of the city's massive public school bureaucracy. With so little money, these schools do not have fancy buildings and play-grounds. Indeed, private school parents reported fewer facil-ities and programs at their child's school than public school parents did.

The Benefits of Competition

All schools perform better in areas where there is vigorous competition among public and private schools. Areas with many low-cost private school choices score 2.7 national per-centile points higher in 8th grade reading; 2.5 national per-centile points higher in 8th grade math; 3.4 national percentile points higher in 12th grade reading; and 3.7 national per-centile points higher in 12th grade math. In short, both tradi-tional forms of choice—choice among school districts and be-tween public and private schools—influence public schools in a positive manner.

Caroline Minter Hoxby, *Education Next*, Winter 2001.

Yet private school parents also reported much higher lev-els of school satisfaction than their public school peers. Pri-vate school parents also were more likely to report that their child had smaller schools, smaller classes and an education-friendly environment (less fighting, cheating, property de-struction, truancy, tardiness and racial conflict). Their chil-dren had more homework and the schools were more likely to communicate with the family. Nor were the private schools any more segregated than the public ones. There was no evidence that vouchers improved the test scores of students from other ethnic groups, however. Vouchers did not have a significant impact, positive or negative, on the test scores of either whites in Dayton of Latinos in New York City. These findings are all the more important, be-cause they come from randomized field trials similar to the pill-placebo trials conducted in medical research, generally regarded as the gold standard of scientific research. Yet the results from these randomized field trials do not so much break new ground as confirm findings from other studies. In a review of the broad range of research, Jeffrey Grogger and Derek Neal, economists from the University of Wisconsin and University of Chicago, find that "urban minorities in Catholic schools fare much better than similar students in public schools," but the effects for urban whites and suburban students generally are "at best mixed."

It is little wonder that many African-Americans are among those most eager to find alternatives to traditional neighborhood public schools. Even though many civil rights leaders oppose school choice, a majority of their constituents think otherwise. In 2000, the Joint Center for Political and Economic Studies reported that 57 percent of African-American adults favored vouchers, as compared with 49 percent of the overall population.

The Quality of Voucher Students

If students who attend private schools seem to benefit thereby, how about those students left behind in traditional public schools? To answer this question, one needs to consider the students in the voucher program, the academic impact on public schools and the financial impact on public schools. Do vouchers attract the best and the brightest?

My own research has looked at this question in two different ways. In one study, my colleagues and I compared a cross-section of all those who applied for a voucher offered nationwide by the Children's Scholarship Fund with a comparable group of those eligible to apply. African-American students were twice as likely to apply as others. Specifically, 49 percent of the applicants were African-American, even though they constituted just 26 percent of the eligible population. Other results reveal little sign that the interest in vouchers is limited to only the most talented. On the contrary, voucher applicants were just as likely to have a child who had a learning disability as non-applicants. Additionally, participants were only slightly better educated than non-applicants.

In New York, Washington, D.C., and Dayton, my colleagues and I found no evidence that private schools' admission policies discriminated on the basis of a young student's test score performance. Only among older students (grades 6–8) in Washington, D.C., did we see some signs that private schools expected students to meet a minimum educational standard prior to admission.

Other researchers find much the same pattern. In Milwaukee, the Wisconsin Legislative Audit Bureau found that the ethnic composition of the participants in Milwaukee's voucher program during the 1998–99 school year did not differ materially from that of students remaining in public schools. Also in Cleveland, Indiana University analysts said that voucher "students, like their families, are very similar to their public school counterparts."

Upon reflection, these findings are not particularly surprising. Families are more likely to want to opt out of a school if their child is doing badly than if that child is doing well. A number of families, moreover, select a private school because they like the religious education it provides, or because it is safe, or because they like the discipline. When all these factors operate simultaneously, the type of student who takes a voucher usually does not look different from those who pass up the opportunity, except perhaps for the fact that those within a specific religious tradition are more likely to choose schools of their own faith.

Public Schools Will Not Suffer

If vouchers do not simply pick off the top students within the public schools, but attract instead a broad range of students, then there is no obvious educational reason why public schools should suffer as a result of the initiative. On the contrary, public schools, confronted by the possibility that they could lose substantial numbers of students to competing schools within the community, might well pull up their socks and reach out more effectively to those they are serving. Interestingly enough, there is already some evidence that public schools do exactly that.

Harvard economist Caroline Minter Hoxby has shown, for example, that since the Milwaukee voucher program was established on a larger scale in 1998, it has had a positive impact on public school test scores. The public schools in the low-income neighborhoods most intensely impacted by the voucher program increased their performance by a larger amount than scores in areas of Milwaukee and elsewhere in Wisconsin not affected by the voucher program.

Even the threat of a voucher can have a positive effect on test scores. Research by Manhattan Institute scholar Jay Greene shows that when public schools were in danger of failing twice on the statewide Florida exam, making their students eligible for vouchers, these public schools made special efforts to avoid failure. . . .

No Religious Divisions

Whatever the advantages of vouchers, some may feel that they would prove divisive in a pluralist society with multiple religious traditions. In his dissent from the majority opinion in *Zelman*, Justice Stephen Breyer saw the decision as risking a "struggle of sect against sect." And Justice John Stevens said he had reached his decision by reflecting on the "decisions of neighbors in the Balkans, Northern Ireland, and the Middle East to mistrust one another. . . . [With this decision] we increase the risk of religious strife and weaken the foundation of our democracy."

These dissents echo the concerns of many distressed by the worldwide rise in fundamentalist religious conviction, worries that have intensified since [the September 11, 2001, terrorist attacks]. But though the concerns are genuine enough, it's hardly clear that government-controlled indoctrination of young people is the best tool for conquering intolerance. On the contrary, this strategy proved counterproductive in many parts of the former Soviet Union.

Historically, the United States has achieved religious peace not by imposing a common culture but by ensuring that all creeds, even those judged as dangerous by the enlightened, have equal access to democratic processes. . . .

The controversies over religion seem more heated in the political and legal world than in the classroom, however. While exceptional cases can always be identified; there is little evidence that religious schools typically teach intolerance. Indeed, careful studies have shown that students educated in Catholic schools are both more engaged in political and community life and more tolerant of others than public school students. After enduring harsh criticism from critics in a Protestant-dominated America, Catholic schools took special pains to teach democratic values. The more recently established Christian, Orthodox Jewish and Muslim schools can be expected to make similar attempts to prove they too, can create good citizens.

As Justice Sandra Day O'Connor pointed out in her concurring opinion, if Breyer and Stevens' fears were real, we would know it already. She showed that taxpayer dollars flow to religious institutions in multiple ways—through Pell Grants to sectarian colleges and universities; via child care programs in which churches, synagogues and other religious institutions may participate; and through direct aid to parochial schools of computers and other instructional materials. If thriving religious institutions create a Balkanized country, she seems to say, this would already have happened.

Nor, say voucher proponents, have public schools eliminated social divisions. As Clarence Thomas argued in his concurring opinion, "The failure to provide education to poor urban children perpetuates a vicious cycle of poverty, dependence, criminality and alienation that continues for the remainder of their lives. It society cannot end racial discrimination, at least it can arm minorities with the education to defend themselves from some of discrimination's effects." In other words, vouchers may help heal, not intensify, the country's most serious social division.

"Voucher schools don't have to follow the same rules of accountability as public schools."

Vouchers Do Not Benefit Urban Students

Barbara Miner

In the following viewpoint Barbara Miner argues that voucher programs will not ensure better educations for most urban students. She asserts that in addition to often being substandard in quality, many private schools place restrictions on the types of students they will admit and use textbooks that are laced with antigay and antiwomen sentiments. Miner concludes that instead of helping urban students, voucher programs do little more than drain money away from already beleaguered public schools. Miner is a writer who specializes in educational issues.

As you read, consider the following questions:

1. What does the author believe is the goal of the voucher movement?
2. According to Miner, what percentage of Milwaukee's voucher schools were either not accredited or not seeking accreditation during the 1998–1999 school year?
3. How do vouchers drain money from public schools, in the author's opinion?

Jennifer Morales thinks of herself as the mother of 100,000 children. Yet only two of them are her birth children. Morales, 33, is the first Latina member of the Board of School Directors of the Milwaukee Public Schools. She views her public policy work as a logical extension of raising her two sons, nine-year-old Anansi and seven-year-old Cedro.

The Concern of One Mother

"A good public education system echoes a lot of the characteristics of good parenting," she said recently over a cup of coffee, between rushing from her son's doctor appointment to City Hall and later to a school board meeting. "It accepts children's differences, it meets the needs of all children, it develops shared values and a sense of responsibility for the broader community, and it teaches essential information and skills."

Milwaukee is home to the country's oldest school voucher program. Morales, like many people involved in schools here, often finds herself caught in one of the nation's key educational controversies: Should public tax dollars be used to fund private schools, including religious schools?

Morales wearies of the question—there is so much that needs to be done to improve public schools, from finding enough money to ensuring smaller classes to tackling the city's high poverty rate. Vouchers, she argues, ignore such crucial issues and call instead for people to abandon their commitment to public education and to the shared institutions that form the heart of our increasingly diverse democracy.

"I never blame parents who move their child from a public school to a private, because it may meet their child's needs," Morales points out. "Just because we have strong shared institutions doesn't mean you have to take part in them. But the public schools serve, and will continue to serve, the majority of children. And just as I want to make schools better for my own children, as a member of the community, I have a responsibility to look out for other people's children as well."

The nation's first voucher program began in Milwaukee in 1990; parents here have a long history with the controversy. Under the voucher program, public tax dollars fund private education for almost 12,000 low-income Milwaukee children, most of whom attend religious schools. A similar program exists in Cleveland, and limited statewide programs exist in Florida and Colorado. A US Supreme Court ruling in the summer of 2002 upheld the legality of public dollars for religious schools, and now, across the country, voucher proposals crop up with increasing frequency. While most proposals target low-income children, the ideological architects of the voucher movement make clear that their goal is a universal system in which vouchers are given to all—in essence, a system in which public schools become increasingly marginal and irrelevant.

Legal Protections Are Ignored

Supporters of public education note that vouchers turn back the clock on more than a half century of efforts to provide legal protections for those previously marginalized—from Title IX prohibitions against gender-based discrimination to the right to a bilingual education to protections for students with disabilities to the demand that public schools respect the rights of gay and lesbian students. In all these areas, voucher schools—by virtue of being private rather than public institutions—can circumvent or ignore hard-won protections. In the long run, establishing two school systems—one public, one private, yet both supported with tax dollars—will only expand the ability of private schools to choose the most desirable students and widen the gap between the haves and the have-nots. This might help a small number of children and parents, but at the expense of the majority of families with school-age children.

For parents in Milwaukee, one of the key complaints is that voucher schools don't have to follow the same rules of accountability as public schools in a broad range of areas: from the services they must provide to the release of information to the public to the quality and certification of teachers. In Milwaukee, accountability is so lax that the state has not collected academic data from voucher schools for more than seven years.

Saphronia Purnell, a 39-year-old mother of three children ages 14 to 18, works with the community-based education reform group Milwaukee Catalyst. An African American, she is well aware that public schools often fail children of color. Her advice? Fight to improve the public schools.

"I don't see vouchers as solving the problems," she says. "My concern is the accountability piece—there doesn't appear to be enough accountability with vouchers, if any at all. A lot of the things required by [the Milwaukee public schools] are not required by the voucher program, and that is a huge concern."

Discrimination Is a Problem

Milwaukee parents have more than a decade of experience to explain why they are wary of vouchers. While there are slight differences in voucher proposals and programs across the country, here are the key issues to be concerned about, based on the experiences of Milwaukee parents:

A private school may not want to educate your child. If your child has exceptional educational needs or speaks English as a second language, you should be concerned. Private schools are not required to provide the same services as public schools. In Milwaukee, for example, only 7 of the 86 participating voucher schools provided special educational services in the 1998-1999 school year—the only year for which there are even minimal academic data about the voucher program, due to a one-time-only report by the state's Legislative Audit Bureau. According to that report, only about 2 percent of voucher students had been previously identified by the public schools as requiring special services. In contrast, about 15 percent of Milwaukee's public school students received special-education services that year. Further, most of the special-education students in the private schools had far less severe problems.

Many private Milwaukee schools are quite explicit that they will not serve special-education students. The Mount Calvary Lutheran School, for instance, indicates that it "is unable to serve students who are unable to climb stairs, have severe emotional problems, are mentally disabled, or have other severe learning problems." St. Bernadette School will not serve students who are more than a year below grade level. Messmer High School, the main private voucher high school, explicitly notes that it has "no special ed classes." As for bilingual education, in 1998–1999 only 2 of the 86 voucher schools provided services for students who did not speak English as a first language.

A private school may not offer the legal protections given to public school students. There has been strong controversy in Wisconsin over the refusal of voucher schools to sign an agreement to abide by basic protections afforded public school students in the areas of free speech and due process, or by state laws prohibiting discrimination on the basis of sex, sexual orientation, pregnancy, or marital or parental status. (State laws already prohibit voucher schools from discriminating on the grounds of race, religion, color, and national origin.)

On a national level, there is particular reason to be concerned about vouchers and the rights of women and gay and lesbian students, particularly since most voucher schools are religiously based. It is not just whether the rights of women and gay and lesbian students will be respected, but whether there is active promotion of homophobic and antifemale attitudes. Many fundamentalist religious textbooks routinely promote intolerance toward gay people and undermine the rights of women. With vouchers, public tax dollars can be used to pay for such textbooks.

Consider this rather typical statement from a high school current-events textbook published by Bob Jones University Press: "[Gay] people have no more claim to special rights than child molesters or rapists." The publisher's civics books also link homosexuality to abortion and say that neither deserves any legal protections.

Academic Performance Is Inconsistent

Vouchers may not lead to a better education for your child. No one knows whether voucher students are performing better, worse, or about the same as Milwaukee's public school students because private schools are not required to release such data. As the Legislative Audit Bureau pointedly noted in its report, "Some hopes for the [voucher] program—most notably that it would increase participating pupils' academic achievement—cannot be documented." One problem is that voucher schools, unlike public schools, are not required to give standardized tests. Even when they do, private schools are not required to release the scores.

Students with academic and disciplinary problems may face particular difficulties. While voucher schools in Milwaukee are not allowed to prohibit admission based on grades or previous discipline records, there are no protections once the child is enrolled; students who do not conform to the private school's standards can be asked to leave. Invariably, they return to the public schools.

The Financial Impact of Vouchers

Vouchers end up costing taxpayers more—for administration and to pay the costs of students not formerly served in public schools.

Milwaukee

By 1998–99, about 6,000 Milwaukee students received vouchers worth about $5,000 each for a total cost of about $29 million. This created a net loss of $22 million to the public schools. . . .

Private scholarships

Even private scholarship programs can reduce funds available for public schools, especially when students use such scholarships initially but then return to public schools mid-year. A September 2000 study by [government professor] Paul Peterson found that about half the students who received private scholarships in Dayton, Ohio, New York City, and Washington, D.C., were back in the public schools by the second year of the program.

Edgewood School District in San Antonio, Texas, provides an illustration of the financial impact of private scholarships. More than 800 students used $4,000 scholarships to attend private and parochial schools—and the Edgewood district lost $5,800 for each student who left. Since students left from a wide array of schools and grades—and given the large number who returned to public schools the loss of $4.8 million caused numerous disruptions and diminutions in the quality of education for public school students.

Michael Pons, "School Vouchers: The Emerging Track Record," www.nea. org, April 2002.

The available evidence points to a private school system that includes good schools, mediocre schools, and substandard schools. In 1998–1999, 28 percent of Milwaukee's voucher schools were neither accredited nor seeking accreditation. Nor were they subject to any independent review of educational quality. Controls are so loose that in 2000 it was revealed that the CEO of a voucher school had been convicted of raping a woman at knifepoint; the information came out only when he was in court on tax-fraud charges stemming from a treatment center for juveniles he had started and later closed. In sentencing the man to six months in jail, Circuit Court Judge Elsa Lamelas pointedly said that the voucher program is set up so "that it is easy pickings for people who are not inclined to be honest."

Voucher schools may not provide sufficient data for parents to make informed decisions. Milwaukee voucher schools do not have to publicly release data about test scores, suspension and expulsion rates, teacher certification, or teacher salaries. They are not required to hire college graduates as teachers. If a parent prefers that his of her child attend an integrated school with a diverse student body, it's not easy to get information on the racial breakdown of voucher schools, which aren't required to release such data.

Vouchers drain money and support from public schools. In an era of declining state economies, school finances are particularly precarious. While every state has different funding mechanisms for public schools, the bottom line is that there is a political limit to how much taxpayers will pay for schools, public or private. Thus, vouchers inherently drain money away from public schools. Equally important, they siphon off support for much-needed reforms such as small classes, improved teacher training, more challenging curricula, and funding equity so that urban and rural schools receive money on a par with more affluent suburban districts.

Since its inception more than a decade ago, more than $250 million has been spent on vouchers in the Milwaukee program, while each year the public schools have faced millions of dollars in budget cuts." In the 2003–2004 school year, the cuts are so severe that all but the bare essentials are being eliminated from some schools—no more teachers of music, art, or physical education. Class sizes are being increased for core academic subjects; in some high schools it is not unusual for a classroom to have more students than desks.

A Dangerous Experiment

Judy Thorsheim, a 56-year-old nurse and mother of three children ranging from 12 to 17 years old, has long been active in her children's schools, from parent-teacher organizations to school-based governance councils. She also works with the religiously based Milwaukee Inner City Congregations Allied for Hope, which focuses on three key policy issues: reforming school funding, providing in-state college tuition for undocumented students who complete high school in Wisconsin, and treatment instead of prison for drug offenders.

Like many others, Thorsheim believes that school funding reform is absolutely essential so that poor districts, which tend to be concentrated in urban and rural areas, have sufficient resources to provide quality education to all children.

"Providing a sound basic education, as the Wisconsin constitution mandates, is the basis of a democracy—everything from being able to vote intelligently to serving on a jury," Thorsheim underscored recently over a breakfast of eggs and hash browns, her fork punctuating the air for emphasis. "How can one discuss and evaluate complicated issues that come up in a jury trial, from DNA evidence to psychological testing, without a good education?"

Thorsheim's advice to parents in communities debating vouchers: "Don't do it. Vouchers are an untested experiment without any controls."

One of the frustrations of parent activists in Milwaukee is that because vouchers have been marketed as "choice," many people don't appreciate the threat that they pose. Who can disagree that public schools, especially in urban areas, fail too many students? But it would be shortsighted to abandon public education and accept the myth that vouchers and privatization are the answer. Public education has tried to fulfill our vision of a more democratic America with institutions responsible to and controlled by the public. The voucher movement betrays that vision. It treats education as a mere consumer item and asks us to settle for the "choice" to apply to a private school that, in the long run, does the choosing.

Morales, Purnell, and Thorsheim admit that the rhetoric of choice is very appealing. But they know that vouchers are not so much about choice as about allowing private schools to operate privately with public dollars, without a commitment to the broader common good.

Former teacher Frank McCourt, author of *Angela's Ashes* and *'Tis*, put it eloquently. Asked in a *New York Times* interview if he would be in favor of vouchers, he replied, "Only if you want to kill public education. That sucking sound you hear is the sound of public schools collapsing with the voucher system."

"For many school districts, the most difficult challenge is hiring and keeping qualified teachers to teach in high-poverty city schools."

Retaining Quality Teachers Will Improve Urban Schools

Scott Joftus and Brenda Maddox-Dolan

Urban schools need to retain experienced teachers if they want their students to receive quality educations, Scott Joftus and Brenda Maddox-Dolan argue in the following viewpoint. According to the authors, the departure of qualified teachers from schools located in high-poverty urban neighborhoods results in students being taught by instructors who lack relevant academic knowledge. Joftus and Maddox-Dolan assert that school districts must develop viable strategies to retain quality teachers. Joftus is the policy director for the Alliance for Excellent Education, and Maddox-Dolan is a policy research associate. The alliance is a national policy and advocacy organization that focuses on the quality of education for low-performing students.

As you read, consider the following questions:
1. According to the authors, why are many experienced teachers leaving schools?
2. What percentage of classes in high-poverty middle schools are taught by instructors who lack a major in the subject they teach, as stated by Joftus and Maddox-Dolan?
3. In the view of the authors, what message does the loss of teachers send?

The new federal No Child Left Behind Act of 2001 (NCLB) requires that all teachers must be "highly qualified," as defined differently in individual states, by the 2005–06 school year. The Alliance [for Excellent Education] believes that NCLB's strong focus on teacher quality is appropriate; compelling research shows that of all the factors that contribute to students' academic achievement, the quality of their teachers is the most important. For example, University of Tennessee researchers W.L. Sanders and J.C. Rivers have found that, within grade levels, the most dominant factor affecting student academic gain was the effect of the teacher, and that this effect increased over time.

As a result, groups of students with comparable abilities and initial achievement levels may have "vastly different academic outcomes as a result of the sequence of teachers to which they are assigned." Perhaps most importantly, the residual effects of both very successful and very unsuccessful teachers are still evident two years later, regardless of the quality of the teachers in the intervening grades.

Urban Schools Are Losing Teachers

When the federal government passed NCLB, one of the goals was to reach out to the students in this country who are most at risk. However, in the very effort of trying to implement NCLB, many school districts, especially those in low-income urban areas, are inadvertently alienating experienced and qualified teachers and not adequately supporting teachers just beginning their careers. In short, these schools are losing—or never had—the very resource they need to make NCLB work.

Many experienced teachers are currently leaving the profession because of low pay, difficult working conditions, and a lack of support from school administrators. With the focus on increased testing as mandated by NCLB, some veteran teachers have begun to feel that they are suddenly much more accountable for student progress while, at the same time, their individual creativity as teachers is no longer valued. With their departure, districts must sometimes hire large numbers of underqualified or beginning teachers to fill the vacancies, and they often do so without putting necessary support systems in place. In addition, schools lose access to veteran teachers' ability both to effectively teach in classrooms and to help create a positive and supportive school culture for new educators.

As a result, the very precondition necessary to ensure that no child is left behind—that is, students' consistent access to qualified and effective teachers—is not now being met. School districts across the country are simply unable to find the high-quality teachers they need, even as they prepare to fill approximately two million teaching vacancies in the coming decade. At the same time, the passage of NCLB has accelerated the new push for qualified teachers, as states hold schools accountable for raising student achievement as measured by test scores.

Disparity in Teacher Quality

Poor urban schools have been hardest hit. For many school districts, the most difficult challenge is hiring and keeping qualified teachers to teach in high-poverty city schools ("high poverty" is defined as an area in which half or more of the students qualify for free or reduced-price lunch). This problem [according to former secretary of education Michael Riley] has resulted in some principals just throwing "a warm body into the classroom, closing the door and hoping for the best."

Nationally, classes in high-poverty secondary schools are 77 percent more likely to be assigned an "out-of-field" teacher—a teacher without experience in the subject they will teach—than classes in "low-poverty" schools (where 15 percent or fewer qualify for free and reduced-price lunch).

Although the disparity is significant in both middle schools and high schools, it is most acute at the middle school level: whereas 29 percent of classes in high-poverty high schools are taught by teachers lacking a major in the subject they teach, 53 percent of classes in high-poverty middle schools are led by such a teacher. Despite common perception, the problem is not only severe in the areas of math, science, and special education, but also in the subjects of English and history.

Research has shown that a firm knowledge of the subject they teach is one of the teacher characteristics that increase student achievement, but the high demand for teachers, coupled with the low supply, is forcing many educators to teach academic subjects for which they have very little background knowledge. It should come as no surprise, then, that many of the young people in high-poverty schools fail to graduate from high school.

The problem of underprepared teachers serving the largest numbers of poor and minority students begins with recruitment. High-achieving, affluent school districts seldom have any trouble hiring qualified, effective teachers and administrators. School systems with high concentrations of poor and minority students, on the other hand, must generally choose from much smaller pools of qualified applicants.

Why Teachers Leave

Teachers who do end up in low-performing schools often don't stay long, creating a "hole in the bucket" that recruiters must try desperately to fill. Since beginning teachers leave the profession at rates five times higher than those of more experienced colleagues, helping new teachers become veteran teachers is an important step in addressing teacher shortages.

Overall, 12 to 20 percent of teachers leave the classroom in their first year, and the rates are even higher in urban and high-poverty schools. (For example, before implementing a support program for new teachers, schools in the urban, high-poverty city of Columbus, Ohio, lost between 20 and 32 percent of their new teachers each year.)

Schools that have trouble attracting teachers in the first place have an especially difficult time holding on to them once they've been hired. Such schools are nearly twice as likely to have higher than average rates of teacher turnover. Teachers in schools with minority enrollments of 50 percent or more, for instance, leave their positions at twice the rate of teachers in schools with relatively few minority students. Teachers give various reasons for leaving their jobs: some leave the profession altogether, some move to other school districts, and some transfer to other schools within the district. Certainly, many teachers also leave their jobs for financial reasons; in 2002, Cynthia Prince of the American

Association of School Administrators found numerous examples of teachers crossing district and even state lines for higher salaries.

Successful Recruitment

One of the most effective ways to provide urban schools with high-quality teachers is to focus recruitment upon individuals who already live and work in urban areas or who have previous experience to prepare them for the particular challenges of urban teaching. For example, urban special education and bilingual paraprofessionals have proven to be a great source of teachers in these two shortage areas, and many cities operate some of their largest and most successful alternate routes for candidates from these backgrounds. . . .

Recruiting teacher candidates from specific populations often requires providing preparation programs that differ substantially from traditional four- or five-year university-based programs. Working and/or retired individuals often already have a college degree or relevant work experience, work full- or part-time, have families, and want to begin teaching as soon as possible. Consequently, successful programs to prepare urban teachers often include substantial financial aid, child care, credit for previous college course work, flexible class scheduling, classes held on-site in local district buildings, and paid internships in lieu of student teaching.

Carla Claycomb, *State Education Standard*, Winter 2000.

However, most teachers don't cite money as their primary reason for entering the profession, and it is also not the main reason they leave. The Southern Regional Education Board has reported that while salary concerns almost always rank among the top few reasons teachers quit (it is cited by 14 percent of responding teachers), "lack of support in schools" (20 percent) and "personal reasons" (29 percent) typically rank higher. Moreover, as shown in that study, educators in their first years of teaching were most likely to cite a lack of support, such as mentoring by experienced teachers, as the primary reason for leaving.

In a National Bureau of Economic Research paper, E.A. Hanushek, J.F. Kain, and S.G. Rivkin concur, arguing that hard-to-staff schools struggle to recruit and keep high-quality teachers because those districts fail to provide effective training, valuable induction programs, and a generally supportive teaching environment. One novice teacher compares the frustration of teaching with no support from her school or district to "a journey for which there is no map to guide you."

This journey is made more perilous by the increased use of high-stakes testing and assessments. As a consequence of these tests, teachers are bearing the primary responsibility for ensuring that students meet standards and pass the assessments.

Many teachers—some of whom are philosophically opposed to the assessments or believe that they take the enjoyment and creativity away from teaching—are leaving the profession as a result. One study found that large numbers of experienced educators who had stopped teaching ranked the pressures of increased accountability—high-stakes testing, test preparation, and standards—as their primary reason for leaving.

A Disastrous Message

The inability to hire and keep the most qualified teachers is more than just a headache for school administrators.

The loss of these teachers sends a powerful—and disastrous—message to students, as well as other faculty members. It signals that the school doesn't have what it takes to be successful: if the most dedicated and effective teachers are unwilling to stay in the school, students—and other teachers in the system, especially those who are underqualified—often become less committed themselves, and may feel a greater sense of discouragement and failure. The entire culture of the school suffers—and with it, the success of its students.

If we are committed to making sure that no child is left behind, school districts across the country will need to develop successful strategies both to support new teachers and to keep veteran educators in place, especially in urban and low-income areas. In short, much more needs to be done to make sure that, regardless of where they teach and how long they've been teaching, no teacher is left behind.

"Afterschool programs can reduce juvenile crime and violence and other risky behaviors by providing alternative environments and activities from 3 P.M. to 6 P.M."

After-School Programs Can Improve the Lives of Urban Teenagers

Georgia Hall, Laura Israel, and Joyce Shortt

In the following viewpoint Georgia Hall, Laura Israel, and Joyce Shortt contend that after-school programs for urban teenagers help contribute to the positive development of these adolescents. According to the authors, these programs can offer a wide range of activities, from jobs and apprenticeships to charity work to socializing, The authors conclude that in order for after-school programs to succeed, community collaboration is vital. Hall is a research scientist, Israel is a research intern, and Shortt is codirector at the National Institute on Out-of-School Time, an organization that seeks to ensure that all children have access to high-quality programs during nonschool hours.

As you read, consider the following questions:
1. According to the authors, what is the most effective way to recruit teenagers into after-school programs?
2. What are the benefits of youth involvement in philanthropic activities, in the authors' view?
3. Why do Hall, Israel, and Shortt believe it is valuable to know the patterns of funding for youth services?

Georgia Hall, Laura Israel, and Joyce Shortt, "It's About Time!: A Look at Out-of-School Time for Urban Teens," National Institute on Out-of-School Time, February 2004. Copyright © 2004 by the National Institute on Out-of-School Time. Reproduced by permission.

There is solid consensus among researchers, program providers, and families that participation in constructive activities during out-of-school time hours can contribute to a high school age youth's healthy and positive development. Research shows that teenagers consistently experience higher levels of motivation and cognitive engagement in youth activities than in other contexts of their lives. . . . Many characteristics of high quality afterschool programs such as youth leadership, communication, and problem-solving activities correlate with the components of the 21st Century learning and literacy skills as outlined by the 1991 SCANS (Secretary's Commission on Achieving Necessary Skills) report and the No Child Left Behind Act of 2001. Research has demonstrated that afterschool programs can reduce juvenile crime and violence and other risky behaviors by providing alternative environments and activities from 3 P.M. to 6 P.M., the prime time for violent juvenile crime. The challenge to city leaders and program providers is creating and sustaining programs and collaborations that engage the interest and participation of high school age youth, and at the same time promote positive developmental outcomes and address the educational needs of the 21st century. . . .

Developing Successful Programs

There is strong consensus from afterschool leaders regarding components of effective high school age youth programs. Teen programs cannot be the same as middle school programs; there are certain fundamental differences between what both populations need and want. The characteristics and capabilities of the youthworker are paramount to program success, and programs for high school age youth are most successful when youthworkers are creative, well trained, skilled at building relationships, and can make long-term commitments to programs.

Finding and retaining the right staff is critical to helping youth participants develop and sustain an interest in program participation. Many programs strive to engage young people initially on a social level through interactions with staff. Once engaged, the programs then offer teens high yield learning opportunities such as computer and music technology.

Program recruitment strategies vary. Teens are often reluctant to reply to flyers, make inquiry phone calls, or pursue website investigation. What seems most effective for high school age youth is direct recruitment within school settings through contact with trusted adults.

In general, programs appear to be most successful in reaching high school age youth and sustaining their interest when:

• Older youth feel a sense of independence as part of participation in the program, particularly financial independence through earning wages or a stipend.

• Youth voices are listened to and incorporated in decision-making.

• Programs offer employable skills, such as office work skills, and include preparation for or direct connection to job training and employment.

• Youth have opportunity to interact with community and business leaders.

• Schools and principals are active partners.

• Participation includes receiving assistance in navigating the post high-school experience.

• Youth are introduced to the world outside their local neighborhood.

The program approaches described in this section offer a range of activities and services to high school age teens. Some of the approaches are initiated by or partnered with city mayoral offices while others are managed by community-based or other non-profit organizations. In choosing which approaches to highlight we were primarily interested in the variation of management structures, goals of the program, variety of incentives to participation, and likelihood of replication. These approaches seemed to "fit well" with the effective program characteristics previously outlined. These programs surfaced numerous times in our investigations and seem to reflect practices that were successful in engaging and supporting high school age youth.

Youth Apprenticeships

In Chicago, Denver, and Boston public/private partnerships have taken on significant roles in promoting and supporting opportunities for high school age youth through the model of Youth Apprenticeships. Youth apprenticeship programs use the workplace as a learning environment to provide youth with competencies in specific work skills and related school skills. After School Matters (ASM) is a non-profit organization that partners with the City of Chicago, the Chicago Public Schools, the Chicago Park District, and the Chicago Public Library to expand out-of-school opportunities for Chicago teens by offering teens hands-on job training in the arts, sports, technology, and communications.

Diversity and Quality

The Beacon centers [an after-school program in San Francisco], provided diverse programming in five core areas: arts and recreation, education, career development, health and leadership development. The centers provided a broad array of activities within and across these activity types, and youth reported that they experienced high levels of interest and challenge in them. Youths' level of interest in the activities compares favorably to other studies of after-school programs. High levels of youth interest across the centers were probably due both to the diversity of activities offered by the Beacon centers within and across core areas and to the Beacons' success at providing activities attuned to the youths' culture (e.g., hip-hop, dancing and drumming, Web-page design).

Attention to developmental opportunities provided by the range of activities was also important. About half of the many activities provided high levels of developmental opportunities, with another third providing average levels. The overall quality of the programming was important in fostering participation. Youth attended activities more regularly if the adult staff managed and structured them well. Presenting material clearly, ensuring that all young people in the group met with some success in their efforts, and responding firmly, but constructively, to misbehavior among youth were all important to keeping youth involved.

Karen E. Walker and Amy J.A. Arbreton, *After-School Pursuits*, March 2004.

After School Matters provides structured out-of-school time opportunities to teens in over 25 of Chicago's high schools. The program strives to prepare youth for jobs, in addition to providing health and fitness oriented clubs. Youth who participate in ASM apprenticeships receive a 10-

week stipend. Employer/apprenticeship partners include schools, YouthNets (units in the community which coordinate youth services), Chicago Department of Human Services, and other community initiatives. Recently, ASM collaborated with local community-based organizations to hire older youth to mentor younger youth in technology skills. Younger youth begin with pre-apprenticeships that combine hands-on and academic enrichment activities and then later transition to supervised internships that focus on learning skills and producing a product. These steps then lead to actual employment for youth in summer camp programs in which they have responsibility for developing curriculum and activities. Through such initiatives, ASM provides a ladder of opportunity towards job readiness and employment to Chicago youth.

One special strand of the Denver Mayor's youth employment program, "Arts Streets" includes apprenticeships in the arts. Through the arts, the program engages youth in the acquisition of life skills, work place skills, and finds a constructive application for youth creativity. Teaching artists and arts organizations are recruited to mentor and guide youth apprentices in visual, performing, literary and media arts curricula.

Classroom in the Workplace is a partnership of the Boston Private Industry Council, the Boston Public Schools, and local Boston employers. During the summer and school year Boston employer partners provide time and space during the workday for high school students to improve their reading comprehension, writing, and mathematics skills. During the summer, classes are held at the worksite for 90 minutes, 5 days a week for 7 weeks, and are led by a Boston Public School teacher. During the school year, students work part-time after school, and one work session is reserved for class. After the classroom component, students disperse throughout various departments to complete the paid job activities assigned to them. . . .

Encouraging Community Service

Research by the National Research Council (2002) reiterates the importance of youth having opportunity to do things that make a real difference in their community. Involving youth in philanthropy activities can increase youth involvement in community change, promote youth service and giving, and help youth develop into healthy productive adults. The El Pomar Foundation's Youth in Community Service program is an interactive, hands-on, learning-by-doing experience that invites high school students to be a positive force in their communities. Twenty-seven public and private high schools from Denver have participated. High school students utilize in-school and out-of-school time to survey classmates, organize fundraisers, participate in a community service event, and meet as a philanthropic board to award self-raised and matched funds from El Pomar to local non-profits. Program leaders cite the great interest high school youth express in the project. Beyond learning about the local community's needs, the youth feel the "power to do something about it."

Chicago Department of Human Service (CDHS) Youth-Net grant making program has also tapped into the high school youth's leadership and philanthropy interests. Youth-Nets exist in each of Chicago's police districts. The programs conduct peer outreach, provide resources, develop leadership skills, hold community forums, and host culminating events. YouthNets awarded 125 grants, ranging from $200 to $1500, to other youth led groups. Activities that have been supported through grants in previous years include community service projects, youth exposure and exploration projects, neighborhood documentaries, and computer enrichment opportunities. These types of youth-led initiatives give Chicago and Denver youth a voice as well as an opportunity to practice leadership and receive recognition in the community for their contributions.

Teen-Centered Spaces

Teens consistently express to program leaders the desire to have a place where they can gather and have "their kind of fun." One model for such a center is Denver's "The Spot," a youth designed and grant supported drop-in center serving ages 14–24. "The Spot" is open Sunday–Thursday from 5:30 P.M. to 10:30 P.M. and includes computer labs, GED classes, broadcasting studios, guest speaker program, photography lab, and dancing space. The Spot is located in downtown Denver in a gang neutral and easily accessible location.

"Teen Central" takes place in the Burton Barr Central Library in Phoenix and was created "for teen by teens." Five teen focus groups were held and surveys were compiled to design the room and decide what materials would be available. Teens told staff that they wanted a space just for ages 12–18. Teen Central hours are Monday–Thursday 10:00 A.M. to 9:00 P.M. with more hours on Friday, Saturday, and Sunday. Regularly over 100 youth engage each day in a range of activities including individual and group computer work, small group discussions, video watching, and general "hanging out" in the canteen. "Teen Central" and "The Spot" reflect critical features of effective programs purported by youth development researchers, including exposure to caring adults, inclusion of youth voices, and hands-on learning activities. . . .

Steps to Take

Efforts to build a citywide strategy for high school afterschool should build upon the groundwork of leadership and philosophy already in place. In some cities the mayor's office may be best positioned to have a broad convening role, having a visibility and presence already established in the schools and employer community—two key areas of connection for high school age youth. In other cities strong leadership may already be present through a public school system or existing intermediary organization.

There are several important steps in developing a citywide approach. First, leaders and stakeholders need comprehensive information about the current landscape of high school afterschool programs. The landscape map, ideally, would categorize programs by target group served, goals of program, funding stream, and capacity for expansion both in numbers of young people served and in types of programming offered. Other essential steps for citywide planning purposes include: (a) an inventory of key city stakeholders already at the table with a plan to bring in others identified as essential; (b) a historical narrative of the city's (all the sectors/stakeholders) experience and interest in providing high school afterschool; and (c) a documentation of programs and practices that are recognized and identified by providers and consumers as effective (including those identified by sources outside of the city's own stakeholders and experts).

In addition to understanding the landscape of programming available for teens, it is essential to know about the current services and capacity of intermediary organizations that provide training, technical assistance, funding, advocacy for funding and policy, and help build the public's commitment and will to provide teens with the support they need to succeed in school and beyond. These necessary functions may reside within singular organizations or be spread among several agencies. Coalitions of programs sometimes fill this role and need to be seen as stakeholders.

The fiscal and political backdrops are crucial pieces of information that will inform initial strategies and the development of an action plan. It is extremely valuable to have budget sources and patterns of funding for youth services. Knowing that there are budget decreases in many states and localities, and understanding the level of support for youth issues in relation to other community needs is helpful in developing an approach to public support. Knowing and understanding the political atmosphere and relationships is powerful. Garnering the right support at the right time is key to sustainability. Balancing political know-how with community organizing and collaboration building is a delicate balance that requires time, reflection, and committed leadership.

Periodical Bibliography

The following articles have been selected to supplement the diverse views presented in this chapter.

American City & County	"NLC Survey Shows Cities Turning to Curfews," February 2002.
Clint Bolick	"School Choice," *American Enterprise*, April/ May 2003.
John Buntin	"Gangbuster," *Governing*, December 2003.
Margaret Davidson	"Do You Know Where Your Children Are?" *Reason*, November 1999.
Marie Gryphon	"Will Schools Ever Be Free from the Chains of State Control?" *USA Today Magazine*, March 2004.
Caroline Minter Hoxby	"Rising Tide," *Education Next*, Winter 2001.
Bill Lockyer	"Blueprint to Reduce Youth Gang Violence," *Business Journal*, May 2, 2003.
Julianne Malveaux	"School Vouchers: A Wedge Issue for African Americans?" *Black Issues in Higher Education*, December 18, 2003.
Paul E. Peterson and William G. Howell	"Voucher Research Controversy," *Education Next*, Spring 2004.
Ryan Pintado-Vertner and Jeff Chang	"The War on Youth," *ColorLines*, Winter 1999/2000.
Daniel L. Schofield	"Gang Congregation Ordinance: Supreme Court Invalidation," *FBI Law Enforcement Bulletin*, September 1999.
J. Richard Ward Jr.	"Implementing Juvenile Curfew Programs," *FBI Law Enforcement Bulletin*, March 2000.
Tim Wheeler	"Supreme Court Injustice," *Political Affairs*, December 2002.

CHAPTER 4

What Is the Future of Urban America?

Chapter Preface

Throughout its history, the United States has been a nation of immigrants. Many of these immigrants, both in centuries past and today, have settled in urban areas. Today 12 percent of the nation's population is foreign born. New York City and Los Angeles are home to between 25 and 30 percent of America's immigrants, and according to a survey conducted by the U.S. Census Bureau in 1999, 40 percent of the residents of New York City were born outside U.S. borders. The effects immigrants have and will continue to have on urban America is a matter of intense debate. While some people believe immigrants will help strengthen the urban economy, others maintain that these newcomers are likely to contribute little other than violence.

The American Immigration Law Foundation (AILF) is among the organizations that believe immigrants will improve the economic future of urban America. According to AILF, "As 43 million Americans relocate every year, immigrants are stepping in to replenish the populations and work forces of America's major cities, keeping them alive and vibrant." The foundation notes the effects immigrants have had on several urban areas, including Washington, D.C. For example, Washington neighborhoods with significant numbers of immigrants have experienced a greater increase in property values than those neighborhoods with fewer immigrants. In an article written for AILF, "Economic Studies Agree: Immigrants Help Our Economic Boom," Margaret A. Catillaz cites a study by the Federal Reserve Bank of Dallas on additional positive effects urban immigrants have on the economy. According to Catillaz, "The study . . . documents that American consumers and urban areas benefit directly from immigration. Consumers benefit because they buy or use goods and services produced by immigrants. Urban areas benefit because immigrants have revived inner-city neighborhoods nationwide."

Other commentators are not so sanguine about the ways immigrants might change urban America. Heather Mac Donald, an editor at the *City Journal*, acknowledges that some Hispanic immigrants in Southern California have renovated and improved their neighborhoods, but she contends that the immigrant experience for Hispanics in Los Angeles has been largely troubling. In her article "The Immigrant Gang Plague," she argues that these immigrants and children of immigrants are more likely than other adolescents to drop out of school, become teenage mothers, or join gangs. Mac Donald suggests that these troubling statistics are unlikely to change, thus immigration will have a negative affect on American culture. She writes, "Underclass indicators like crime and single parenthood do not improve over successive generations of Hispanics—they worsen. Debate has recently heated up over whether Mexican immigration—unique in its scale and in other important ways—will defeat the American tradition of assimilation." She further opines that Hispanic gang violence will continue to be a problem not only in Los Angeles but also in Chicago, Phoenix, and other cities.

Whether urban America will thrive in the future depends on a number of factors, from demographics to policies on development. In the following chapter the authors offer several predictions about the future of America's cities.

> *"Urban growth boundaries must be complemented by smart land use, transportation, and housing policies."*

Smart-Growth Policies Will Improve Urban Areas

John Fregonese and Lynn Peterson

Smart-growth policies are an approach to urban development that emphasize features such as public transit and high-density developments. In the following viewpoint John Fregonese and Lynn Peterson contend that criticisms of smart-growth policies are unfounded. They assert that smart growth offers numerous benefits to cities, including reduced traffic congestion, more affordable housing, increased employment, and lower tax burdens. Fregonese is an urban planner and Peterson is the manager of strategic planning for the Tri-County Metropolitan Transportation District of Oregon (Tri-Met).

As you read, consider the following questions:
1. According to the authors, what is the median sales price for a house in Portland?
2. How does growth management make homes more affordable, in Fregonese and Peterson's opinion?
3. As stated by Fregonese and Peterson, where does Oregon rank among the fifty states in terms of tax burden?

The Congress for the New Urbanism aims to change the way America builds its cities and towns. We want regions that are made of thriving neighborhoods, connected by efficient, effective transit. We want neighborhoods that feel alive, where people from all walks of life can cross each other's paths and meet their needs. We call this form of development New Urbanism, and the policies that support it are called Smart Growth.

Current development practices create sprawl. For too long, our development system has produced a landscape that is dominated by the private car. Most new developments are miserable to walk in, and impossible to serve with transit. No wonder traffic jams get worse every year.

There is wide support for changing this state of affairs. Tens of millions of Americans want to live in walkable neighborhoods served by transit. However, a cottage industry of "sprawl apologists" has sprung up. This small group of individuals and think tanks aggressively distribute misinformation about New Urbanism and Smart Growth, developing notoriety as defenders of the status quo.

The most frequently quoted individual behind these "Dumb Growth" efforts is Wendell Cox. In his papers, Cox attacks Portland, Oregon, as the epitome of Smart Growth, and uses Atlanta, Georgia, as an example of the high quality of life provided by car-dependent development.

Imitating Portland's policies of urban growth boundaries will not guarantee quality growth or a better transportation system within a metropolitan area. Urban growth boundaries must be complemented by smart land use, transportation, and housing policies. Portland, though imperfect, has created this complex of policies, and the city's residents are currently reaping the benefits.

This paper shows that Portland is doing much better than Cox admits. It demonstrates that many of Cox's statistics are questionable, if not simply false.

Cox's writings have distorted the facts. We aim to correct the record.

Cox claims: From 1990 to 1999 Atlanta's per capita daily VMT [vehicle miles travelled] increased 20.6 percent compared with 28.5 percent in Portland. And, Portland's daily hours of delay will increase, due to transit oriented development, on roadways by 600 percent by 2020.

Error Number 1

This finding is based on a statistic that has since been corrected by its authors.

Cox uses Federal Highway Administration [FHWA] data on population and daily vehicle miles travelled (VMT) for the Portland-Vancouver region. The FHWA has already acknowledged an error in the population estimate for 1999—the agency accidentally reduced the population for the Portland Metro region by approximately 150,000 from 1998. This makes VMT per capita appear to have increased far more than it actually did.

When this error is corrected, the increase in VMT per capita is about 9.6 percent for the combined Portland-Vancouver region over the period 1990–1999, not 28.5 percent. This is less than half the increase found in Atlanta.

Even this number is higher than that from another reputable source. According to the federal Highway Performance Monitoring System, actual VMT increase per capita is only 8.2 percent.

To compare Smart Growth with business as usual, Portland is but one good example. Miami/Dade County, Florida, has also had an urban limit line for 30 years. Both Portland and Miami show dramatically lower overall driving than Atlanta, as well as much slower rates of increase. . . .

These results have led the independent Texas Transportation Institute (TTI) to find, "The rate of growth in traffic congestion is starting to slow, and Portland's long-term attack on transportation problems is starting to give the region an edge over cities that have spent hundreds of millions of dollars on new freeways."

Congestion in Atlanta

Error Number 2

Cox uses the TTI travel time index to claim that Portland and Atlanta are tied in 8th place for congestion. However, TTI's supporting documents say that the Travel Time Index is an intermediate value used to calculate the hours of delay, excess fuel, and congestion cost. It measures average vehicle speed, not the real world effect of congestion. The real picture emerges when time lost in traffic is compared. When Atlanta is compared to other less sprawling regions, it reveals the advantages of a compact area over a sprawling one. . . .

How Federal Governments Can Support Smart Growth

Protect Open Space and Scenic Landscapes. Federal interest in land protection has a long history, but funding has not kept up with demand. From National Parks to wildlife habitat, federal efforts to protect key pieces of land should match the efforts being made at the state and local level. Public officials should also fight to preserve the cherished scenic vistas that make our communities special and drive our growing tourism industry. In particular, the federal government should ease restrictions limiting communities' ability to fight billboard blight.

Refocus Transportation Policy. For the last 50 years, federal transportation policy has focused on highways. A new commitment of federal funding to provide people with alternatives to roads, from reliable bus services to bike lanes, can give communities the boost they need to make these projects happen. More funding should be devoted to improving public transit access between homes and jobs. Also, our federal commitment to the country's unfinished rail systems and greenways should match the commitments made in the past to highways and airports.

Support Housing Programs. The federal government is an important partner in ensuring access to housing for low-income families. The buying power of key federal programs has eroded over time, and our ability to assure adequate housing is falling further behind market needs. The federal government can support housing programs by providing a larger low-income housing tax credit, helping states establish affordable housing trust funds, providing more assistance for subsidized housing, and linking housing to job opportunities through public transportation programs.

Smart Growth America, *Greetings from Smart Growth America*, no date.

Since 1992, Portland's congestion rankings have either remained unchanged or improved slightly. Meanwhile, Atlanta, which in 1992 was 16th nationally in congestion, has shot to the top of the charts.

Atlanta fares much worse than many cities in their rising

cost of congestion. . . . When comparing the annual congestion cost from 1990 through 1999, Portland and Miami have increased far less than Atlanta, showing the advantage of maintaining a compact region in the face of growth.

More Affordable Housing

Cox's Claim: The median price between 1991 and 2000 in Portland rose 110 percent to $168,000; Atlanta's rose 65 percent to $150,000 and nationwide the average rose 49 percent to $152,000.

Error Number 1

Cox' source, the NAHB [National Association of Home Builders] affordability index, overstates the housing affordability problem in Portland. Portland has a median income of $55,900 and median sale price of $168,000, making the ratio of price to income 1 to 3. However, the NAHB gives Portland an affordability score of 40.2. Using a simple ratio of price to income. Portland is more affordable than Santa Barbara, California, where median income is $56,500 and the median sale price is $210,000 (a ratio of 1 to 3.7). However, the NAHB system ranks Santa Barbara as more affordable, with a score of 45.7. Similarly, Denver is ranked much more affordably, with a score of 56.3, even though that city's ratio of income to home price is exactly the same as Portland's.

NAHB index doesn't reflect reality, because its methods are overly abstract. To determine affordability, the NAHB calculates a home mortgage and compares it to the median income in an area. Because mortgage calculations are affected by property taxes and insurance, the abstract model gives some curious results. Oregon's voters have chosen to have high property taxes, in return for having no sales tax. Insurance rates are also higher in Oregon than in many other states. These factors throw off standardized, nationwide calculations.

Intelligent Land Use Regulations

Error Number 2

Cox blames the city's Urban Growth Boundary (UGB) for housing costs, ignoring other factors. While housing in the region did get more expensive for the first few years of the 1990s, *land supply played a very small role in rising costs.*

According to the Oregon Housing Cost Study, the median home price in the Portland area rapidly increased from 1991 to 1998. Yet in looking at specific developments, the increase in raw land costs was only $15,704 of the total increase, less than the $25,317 increase in hard and soft land costs, such as water and sewer lines, utilities, system development charges, and architecture fees. The same held true elsewhere in the state. In Eugene-Springfield, the modest increase in land costs, $1,778, was dwarfed by the increase in the cost of building the house itself, $18,772. In Salem, land costs rose by only $1,542 while hard and soft land costs rose by $21,670 and the cost of building the house rose by $12,791. The only cost a UGB could affect is land cost. Land cost has risen slightly, but other costs are responsible for most of the housing price increase.

Finally, *Oregon's UGB laws do not restrict the amount of available land.* Oregon law requires fast-growing cities, cities with populations over 25,000, and metropolitan service districts to include enough buildable land for the next 20 years of residential growth within their urban growth boundaries (Oregon Revised Statutes, 197.296). *A perpetual 20-year supply of residential land clearly is not a severe limit.*

A joint study by the Home Builders Association of Metropolitan Portland and 1000 Friends of Oregon concluded that Oregon's program of UGBs, in combination with other tools from the land use program, has kept housing prices in the Portland metropolitan area lower than other West Coast cities. This is because the program requires cities to designate land for all types of housing, and because developers wishing to build on that land get one of the fastest permitting processes in the nation.

In 1992, the same group wrote, "Land use regulation can in fact be a powerful force to reduce housing costs and red tape. In Oregon, it has done just that."

Other Benefits of Smart Growth

Error Number 3

Focusing on affordability in 1990 and 2000 ignores the more detailed trend. *Despite an ongoing economic boom, Portland's housing cost increases flattened out after 1995, and now roughly match the rate of inflation.* .... Home prices changed as the UGB was created and the Functional Plan (land use plan for the region) was adopted. In fact, the percent change in home prices stabilized and began to fall as the Functional Plan was adopted. If anything . . . the region's land use rules have been a success. This could be because developers enjoy the stable environment of predictable land use rules. The Oregon system seems able to provide housing reliably, even during boom times.

Error Number 4

Growth management actually helps improve affordability. A Rutgers University study concluded that without a statewide planning act in New Jersey, each new home would cost $12,000 to $15,000 more. Rutgers pegged capital costs attributable to sprawl development patterns at $1.3 billion over 20 years for roads, water, sewer and school facilities. Additional operating and maintenance costs of $400 million annually were linked to sprawl development.

Smart Growth Helps a Region's Economy

Cox's claim: During the 1990s, Atlanta's employment increased 37.3 percent compared with 30.5 percent in Portland. Median household income also increased more dramatically in Atlanta, up 52 percent here from 1990 to 2000 compared with 44.7 percent in Portland.

Error Number 1

Both Portland and Atlanta boomed in the 1990's. *A 30.5 percent increase in employment is not evidence of policies that hurt the economy.* Statewide, Oregon's total employment per capita remained the same throughout the 1990s, at about .5 jobs per capita.

Error Number 2

Growth management has actually helped the Oregon economy considerably.

• Because of growth management, Metro Portland's counties remain in the top 5 nursery producing counties in the state, and have high agricultural output.

• The high usage of transit in the Portland region removes approximately 51.7 million car trips from the regional infrastructure. Transit also allows for more efficient use of land, keeping people closer to their destinations.

Smart Growth Saves Governments Money

Cox's claim: State and local government costs rose 13 percent per capita in Georgia compared with 82 percent in Oregon.

Error Number 1

These numbers are apples and oranges. Oregon's 16.5% increase per biennium between 1991–1993 and 2001–2003 is due to new mandates from its voters. Two thirds of the $6 billion growth came from the voters' shifting the state's education budget from school district property taxes to state income taxes. Another billion came from increased access to health care for moderate and low income Oregonians under Measure 44. Another $290 million came from increased spending on prisons and parkland.

Error Number 2

Smart growth actually saves taxpayers money. According to the non-partisan watchdog group the Tax Foundation, *Oregonians pay lower taxes than do Georgians.* The Tax Foundation looks at both state and local taxes. They find that the tax burden for Oregon is substantially lower than in Georgia. In 2000, Oregon ranked 39th in the nation, while Georgia ranked 27th.

Error Number 3

In fact, sprawl is the system that requires subsidies. In a 1989 monograph for the Urban Land Institute, James Frank, associate professor of urban and regional planning at Florida State [University], estimated a $48,000 per house sprawl "premium" for providing services to a three unit per acre development located ten miles from central facilities and employment centers. By contrast, the same costs for a home in a 12-unit per acre development, located closer in, with an equal mix of townhouses, garden apartments and single family homes, would be 50 percent lower.

| *"Smart growth is about the centralization of power over American lifestyles."*

Smart-Growth Policies Will Harm Urban Areas

Randal O'Toole

In the following viewpoint Randal O'Toole argues that the approach to urban development known as "smart growth," which emphasizes high-density housing and discourages automobiles, creates numerous problems for American cities. He contends that if smart-growth policies are adopted throughout the nation, traffic congestion and housing costs will increase while open spaces will likely disappear. O'Toole is an economist and the director of the Thoreau Institute, an organization that aims to protect the environment without government regulation or bureaucracy.

As you read, consider the following questions:

1. Why will smart growth lead to a decline in home ownership, in the author's view?
2. According to O'Toole, what is the end result of smart-growth policies?
3. What does O'Toole believe should be the role of governments in urban development?

Randal O'Toole, *The Vanishing Automobile and Other Urban Myths: How Smart Growth Will Harm American Cities*. Bandon, OR: Thoreau Institute, 2001. Copyright © 2001 by the Thoreau Institute. Reproduced by permission.

Years before the term *smart growth* had been coined, *Washington Post* writer Joel Garreau asked an urban planner how he would change a low-density urban area. "I would increase dramatically the real residential population," he replied. "Give me 100,000 people . . . not living within a mile or two miles. I want them living right here. I'd raise the gasoline tax by 300 percent. I'd raise the price of automobiles enormously. I mean I would just limit movement . . . and there would be a massive rush to live near your work, your social or commercial activity. And then I would put enormous costs on parking. I think just tak[ing] transportation alone, you could change these places dramatically."

"Given vast powers," comments Garreau, what this planner would do "is force Americans to live in a world that few now seem to value." Today, we recognize the planner's prescription as smart growth: Use transportation policy to immobilize people so that, like nineteenth century urbanites, they will be happy living in high densities.

For more than a century, rising incomes and new technologies have given American urbanites greater choices about where to live and how to travel, and most of them have decided to live in lower density areas and to travel by auto. Now smart-growth planners want to turn back the clock by rebuilding cities to nineteenth-century densities and forcing people to use nineteenth-century transportation technologies. If *sprawl* is defined by auto usage, then the sprawl opponents' idea of a *livable city* is a city with fewer automobiles. "A livable city is one in which you can buy your morning orange juice without driving a car," says Portland's Mayor Vera Katz. "Livable cities occur when all one's needs can be met within walking distance, public transport distances, or short drives," agrees Portland planning advocate Robert Bremmer.

The Reality of Smart Growth

Sometime around 1996, sprawl warriors coined the term *smart growth* to describe their alternative to low-density suburbs. Unlike the terms they previously used, such as *compact cities*, *neotraditionalism*, and *new urbanism*, smart growth has attracted national attention. After all, people will argue about whether they want compact cities or traditional neighbor-

179

hoods, but who will argue in favor of dumb growth or sprawl when a smart-growth alternative is available?

What Is Smart Growth?

As planners describe it, smart growth is an attractive vision of people living and working in pedestrian-friendly communities, walking to the store, taking light rail on longer trips, and using the automobile only as a last resort. As a result, smart growth supposedly allows urban areas to grow without increasing congestion, pollution, taxes, or the loss of open space.

The reality of smart growth is far from th[at] vision:

• Smart growth not only causes congestion, many smart-growth advocates believe that increased congestion is needed to make it work;

• Yet even with increased congestion, smart growth does not lead significant numbers of people to trade in their cars for transit, walking, or cycling;

• Smart growth's effects on air pollution are ambiguous, since the effects of increased congestion on auto emissions are likely to offset the minor reductions in auto driving;

• Similarly, smart growth not only causes single-family home prices to rise, but some smart-growth advocates may believe that such price increases are needed to convince people to live in high-density, transit-oriented developments;

• As a result, rates of home ownership can be expected to decline and low-income people will have a harder time paying for decent housing;

• Far from keeping its promise of reducing urban-service costs, smart growth imposes extra burdens on taxpayers to cover the costs of subsidized rail transit and subsidized high-density housing;

• Smart growth is likely to lead to increased costs for consumer goods due to a reduction in retail competition and an emphasis on small, noncompetitive stores;

• Urban open spaces will rapidly disappear to infill;

• Nor does smart growth guarantee protection of rural open spaces—instead, it may lead to accelerated exurbanization of rural areas;

• finally, smart growth causes a tremendous loss of both freedom and mobility.

Despite these problems, the smart-growth vision is widely shared among the nation's political and urban leaders, led by [former] Vice President Al Gore. Smart-growth supporters include the governors of Oregon, Maryland, Minnesota, and Georgia, among others; the mayors of Albuquerque, Atlanta, Minneapolis, Nashville, Portland, Sacramento, San Diego, Seattle, and many other big cities; editorial writers for such major newspapers as the *Los Angeles Times, Minneapolis Star-Tribune,* the *Portland Oregonian;* and numerous interest groups ranging from the Sierra Club to the National Trust for Historic Preservation, plus of course rail transit builders and other businesses that expect to profit from smart growth.

Asay. © 1998 by Creators Syndicate, Inc. Reproduced by permission.

One place where the vision is *not* supported is in the data produced by the government agencies promoting smart growth. The background data for almost every proposal for higher densities, light rail, transit-oriented development, and other smart-growth proposals show that these plans will lead to increased congestion and declining urban open space. Many of the plans admit that air pollution will get worse, and they inevitably lead to higher housing prices and require higher subsidies and therefore higher taxes.

Growth Will Occur

Smart growth is *not* no growth. Debates over growth vs. no growth that characterized the 1970s were largely won by the growth side. A significant no-growth or slow-growth minority remains, represented by Eban Fodor's recent book, *Better Not Bigger.* Fodor argues that smart growth "fails to address the amount of growth that is desirable." He believes that "we may be able to identify an optimal size for each community, or at least a 'maximum size' beyond which the quality and livability will decline." Although he never says how this optimal size is to be calculated, once it is calculated he argues that smart growth and no growth are "completely compatible and even complementary."

If smart growth really meant no growth, most of smart growth's supporters would abandon the movement. The war on sprawl is fought by a coalition of pro-growth forces in the cities combined with anti-auto, anti-suburb forces among planners and environmentalists. While some sprawl opponents may not like growth, most recognize that accepting growth is necessary to maintain this coalition: The no-growth minority is expected to support smart growth as the lesser of evils.

People on both sides of the smart-growth issue sometimes portray their opponents as no-growth advocates. But most interest groups on both sides accept that growth is not the issue; the question is how we grow. The twin goals of the war on sprawl are to:

• "Grow up, not out"—that is, grow by increasing densities rather than by spreading across the land.

• "Reduce auto dependency" by emphasizing transit and walkable neighborhoods rather than roads and autos.

Smart-growth advocates have a precise idea of what they want American cities to look like in the future. . . . Smart growth consists of five major prescriptions:

1. Significantly increase urban and suburban population densities.

2. Spend scarce transportation dollars on rail transit that few people will ride instead of taking steps that can genuinely relieve traffic congestion.

3. Discourage auto driving by, among other things, man-

dating so-called pedestrian-friendly, but really automobile-hostile, design codes.

4. Redevelop existing neighborhoods into high-density mixed-use, transit-oriented developments.

5. Create regional governments that can impose these policies on reluctant suburbs and neighborhoods with little or no democratic consent.

Taken together, smart-growth policies amount to the immobilization of America. Contrary to its proponents' claims, smart growth does not reduce congestion; it increases it. Privately—and sometimes publicly—smart-growth supporters admit that they consider increased congestion to be a benefit.

The False Claims of Smart Growth

The surprising part is that anyone supports smart growth. Yet smart growth's chief supporters—urban planners and urban environmentalists—have built powerful coalitions with a wide range of other interest groups by portraying smart growth as all things to all people. Are you worried about congestion? Smart growth will get cars off the road. Annoyed by high taxes? Smart growth will save money. Concerned about the future of the inner city? Smart growth will save it. Air pollution, poverty, historic buildings? Smart growth, it is claimed, will fix or save them all. In fact, the opposite is more likely to happen.

Ultimately, smart growth is about power:

• Who gets to decide how you travel and where you live, work, and shop: you, or a government planner who thinks cars are immoral and that you should walk to the grocery store and take mass transit to work?

• Who gets to collect taxes and make land-use decisions in your neighborhood: decentralized local governments or a centralized metropolitan government?

• Who decides how your gasoline taxes and other highway user fees are spent: people interested in promoting mobility, or a government agency that frets and moralizes over people's travel preferences?

• Who will set the agenda for your city's future: local residents or Washington bureaucrats in the Environmental Protection Agency?

Smart growth is about the centralization of power over American lifestyles in an age when nearly every other country in the world has given up on central planning. Smart-growth advocates seek to give regional governments the exclusive power over land-use and transportation planning in urban areas. Under the thumb of the Environmental Protection Agency, which will favor urban areas that follow smart-growth prescriptions with federal funds, these regional governments will force cities to rezone neighborhoods to higher densities and divert highway user fees to transit. . . .

Opponents of smart growth favor instead the decentralization of power and responsibility to local municipalities rather than regional governments; to neighborhoods rather than cities; and to individuals rather than any government authority. Some government services can better be provided by the private sector. Where government is needed, it should respond to public needs and desires, not attempt to manipulate people into changing their behavior to suit bureaucratic whims or misconceptions.

"Until approximately the 1980s, cities and nature were widely viewed as mutually exclusive."

American Cities Will Become More Compatible with Nature

Rutherford H. Platt

Rutherford H. Platt asserts in the following viewpoint that city planners are becoming increasingly aware of the importance of green, natural areas within urban areas. He maintains that "green urbanism," in which city governments and local and environmental organizations provide ecological services such as crop pollination and water purification in urban settings, is occurring in Chicago, New York City, and other major cities. According to Platt, these efforts will benefit cities both environmentally and socially. Platt is a professor of geography and planning law at the University of Massachusetts in Amherst.

As you read, consider the following questions:
1. According to Platt, what suggestions did Ian McHarg make to urban designers?
2. What ecological projects have taken place in Chicago, as stated by the author?
3. What does Platt consider a possible fringe benefit of urban ecological activities?

Rutherford H. Platt, "Toward Ecological Cities: Adapting to the 21st Century Metropolis," *Environment*, June 2004, p. 10. Copyright © 2004 by Helen Dwight Reid Educational Foundation. Originally published in *Land Use and Society* by Rutherford H. Platt. Copyright © 2004 by the author. Reproduced with permission of the Helen Dwight Reid Educational Foundation, published by Heldref Publications, 1319 18th St. NW, Washington, DC 20036-1802 and by Island Press, Washington, DC.

Even as urban design professionals continue to manipulate the physical form and appearance of the built environment, another type of social adaptation to the enveloping metropolis is emerging, one which focuses on the unbuilt elements of the urban environment. Such adjustments are concerned less with the way urban places look and more with the way they function—ecologically and socially. Fundamental to this new perspective are four premises:

• metropolitan regions are essentially inescapable—so we might as well make them as habitable, safe, and pleasant as possible;

• the first premise applies to most metropolitan inhabitants, rich and poor alike;

• the laws of nature are not suspended within urban areas; and

• respecting and restoring natural systems within urban places is often more cost-effective than using technological substitutes.

The incipient urban ecology movement differs from earlier forms of adaptation . . . chiefly in terms of the fourth premise—which implies a more vigorous appreciation of the role of nature and its functions within the metropolis. Here again the land use and society model is validated: Research across the spectrum of natural, physical, and social science offers new insights on the relationship between humans and nature in urban settings. These insights in turn stimulate new strategies to nurture and restore ecological services in urban places. Such approaches have been described variously as green urbanism, green infrastructure, and natural cities, as well as variations of urban sustainability. Building on the book *The Ecological City: Preserving and Restoring Biodiversity*, the term "ecological city" is a convenient descriptor for communities and regions that seek to become more green, more healthy, more efficient, and more socially equitable than conventional urban places. Whatever the term, something new is happening. Until approximately the 1980s, cities and nature were widely viewed as mutually exclusive. [Historian] Lewis Mumford in 1956 deplored the tendency of the modern city: ". . . to loosen the bonds that connect [its] inhabitants with nature and to transform, eliminate, or replace its earth-bound aspects, covering the natural site with an artificial environment that enhances the dominance of man and encourages an illusion of complete independence from nature."

New Perspectives on Cities and Nature

One reason for this illusion has been the professional disdain of natural scientists for cities. For instance, an influential Conservation Foundation book of the mid-1960s, *Future Environments of North America*, virtually ignored urban places—although they were certainly the future environments of most North Americans. In 1971, ecologist Eugene P. Odum viewed cities as being parasitic: "Great cities are planned and grow without any regard for the fact that they are parasites on the countryside, which must somehow supply food, water, air, and degrade huge quantities of wastes." (Many of those functions also can occur within urban areas with appropriate land use allocation.) As recently as 1988, a prominent National Academy of Sciences book, *Biodiversity*, devoted a mere 7 out of 520 pages to "urban biodiversity." The view of nature as existing only beyond the urban fringe or in exotic and distant places accessible only to scientists and the affluent ecotourist is perpetuated by some well-meaning natural history museums, zoos, public aquariums, and television nature documentaries.

The seed of a different perspective on cities and nature was planted by landscape architect Ian McHarg in his seminal 1968 book *Design with Nature*. McHarg urged urban designers to evaluate and incorporate natural factors such as topography, drainage, natural hazards, and microclimate into their plans, rather than overcoming such constraints through technology—which often incurs high costs and has an uneven record of success. McHarg's advice was directed primarily to the planning of new and often upscale suburban development.

However, the proposition would be significantly expanded, geographically and functionally, by fellow landscape architect Anne Whiston Spirn in her 1985 book *The Granite Garden;* "The city, suburbs, and the countryside must be viewed as a single, evolving system within nature, as must every individual park and building within that larger whole. . . . Nature in the city must be cultivated, like a garden, rather than ignored or subdued. In 1987, *The Greening of the Cities* [by David Nicholson-Lord] examined British experience with "cultivating nature in cities," proposing that ecology offers "a way out of manmade aesthetics and proprietorial landscapes." In a more emotional voice, evolutionary biologist Lynn Margulis and her son Dorion Sagan put it this way: "The arrogant habitat-holocaust of today may cease; in its wake may evolve technologically nurtured habitats that rebind, reintegrate, and re-merge us with nature."

Ecological Services

The dawning perception that cities and nature are not mutually exclusive (and that urban ecology is not an oxymoron) did not lead ipso facto to rewriting the ground rules for urban growth and redevelopment. An essential step in that direction was the development of the concept of "ecological services" by biologists Paul Ehrlich and Gretchen Daily and also by the international Scientific Committee on Problems of the Environment. "Ecological services" are benefits nature provides to human society—in both rural and urban settings—including

- purification of air and water;
- mitigation of floods and drought;
- detoxification and decomposition of wastes;
- generation and renewal of soil and soil fertility;
- pollination of crops and natural vegetation;
- control of potential agricultural pests;
- dispersal of seeds;
- maintenance of biodiversity;
- protection from solar ultraviolet rays;
- moderation of urban microclimate (such as the urban heat island effect);
- support for diverse human cultures; and
- aesthetic and intellectual stimulation.

To the extent that these natural functions are disrupted or eliminated by human activities, they often must be replaced through technical substitutes such as flood control, water filtration, irrigation, agricultural chemicals, air conditioning, or sun block. More ecological forms of urban adaptation use nonstructural measures where possible. In place of steel and concrete, greater reliance is placed on law, economics, education, science, the arts, and even spirituality to improve metropolitan habitability. For example, New York City and metropolitan Boston are employing watershed management in preference to building costly filtration plants to protect the quality of their drinking water, an option available under the federal Safe Drinking Water Act.

Parks and Property Values

Parks' value to neighborhood quality is . . . confirmed by studies that find a statistically significant link between property values and proximity to green space, including neighborhood parks and urban forested areas. One study found that the value of properties near Pennypack Park in Philadelphia increased from about $1,000 per acre at 2,500 feet from the park to $11,500 per acre at 40 feet from the park. . . . Another found that the price of residential property—based on data from three neighborhoods in Boulder, Colorado—decreased by $4.20 for every foot farther away from the greenbelt. . . .

This connection between urban parks and neighborhood quality is receiving renewed attention from community developers as they strive to make their neighborhoods more attractive to low-income and, increasingly, middle-income residents.

Chris Walker, "The Public Value of Urban Parks," 2004.

Evaluating the cost-effectiveness of ecological approaches such as the New York watershed management strategy is complicated by the difficulty of assigning monetary values to ecological services. The field of ecological economics, pioneered by Robert Costanza, seeks to develop rough quantitative measures of the monetary value of nature's bounty. However, independent of such a dollars-and-cents approach, the qualitative value of ecological process and biodiversity to a sense of urban place is also gaining influence, as in this statement by urban naturalist Michael W. Klemens:

Biodiversity is inextricably part of our sense of place, the very fabric of our comfort and our "being" at a particular locus. The natural world provides the texture and variety that define where we live, work and play. So defined, biodiversity is the tapestry of colors on a wooded hillside in October, the interplay between water and reeds, the chirping of crickets on a summer's night, the ebb and flow of natural systems evolving over time. And it is that natural template, the very foundation upon which our society is built, that I define as biodiversity, or more simply stated, nature.

Moving Toward Green Urbanism

Unlike large-scale structural projects, "ecological adjustments" are often localized, ad hoc, and informal. According to planner Timothy Beatley, "green urbanism" in European cities includes such elements as green roofs, community gardens, car-free neighborhoods, pavement removal, passive solar heating, and cohousing. Many of these are beginning to appear in American cities at various scales and encompassing a broad spectrum of goals and means. . . . Some strategies that have been identified by the Ecological Cities Project (www.ecologicalcities.org), based at the University of Massachusetts, Amherst, include

- rehabilitation and adaptation of older parks and urban greenspaces;
- protection and restoration of urban wetlands and other sensitive habitat;
- preservation of old growth trees and forest tracts;
- development of greenways and rail trails;
- urban gardening and farm markets;
- green design of buildings, including green roofs and green schools;
- brownfield remediation and reuse;
- urban watershed management;
- riverine and coastal floodplain management;
- endangered species habitat conservation plans;
- urban environmental education sites and programs; and
- environmental justice programs.

Such efforts are typically led by nongovernmental or quasigovernmental organizations such as museums and botanic gardens, schools and colleges, community groups, watershed alliances, regional planning bodies, and local chapters of national organizations like The Nature Conservancy, Trust for Public Land, Sierra Club, and National Audubon Society. Such organizations provide vision, persistence, and sometimes volunteers to work in the field. Public sector agencies at all levels may play supporting roles, providing funding, staff resources, technical know-how, and (where applicable) regulatory muscle. Funds also may be contributed by businesses, foundations, and individuals, especially for projects in localities of particular interest to the donor. Researchers in universities, public agencies, and nongovernmental organizations [NGOs] help to define the scientific and social goals and means.

Ecological Projects in American Cities

Local ecological cities activities are often scattered, uneven, and underfunded. But like ecological organisms, they thrive on diversity: diversity of goals, of means, of participants, of disciplines, and (one hopes) of viewpoints. Some are closely related to parallel movements concerning social and environmental justice, affordable housing, physical fitness, public health, natural disaster mitigation, animal rights, and environmentalism writ large. They depend on spontaneous and often voluntary local leadership. They are pragmatic and creative in stitching together existing program resources, available funding, and donations of money, time, and office space. Most involve public-private partnerships, some of which are local alliances to save a particular site or pursue a single goal, such as environmental education or urban gardening. Others have evolved into influential regional networks such as Chicago Wilderness. . . . The range of ecological cities projects underway or in planning is remarkable. In Chicago alone, under its proactive mayor, Richard M. Daley,

• the City Hall now has an experimental "green roof" with pathways, a beehive, and some 200 species of plants;

• the city, state, and federal government are drawing up an ambitious plan for the economic and ecological revitalization of the vast Calumet Lake industrial zone on the city's South Side;

• planters with native species of grasses and prairie plants are scattered around the central business district;

• urban gardens and neighborhood greenspaces are being established on vacant lots in city neighborhoods; and

• Lake Shore Drive was relocated to create a walkable

"museum campus" bordering Lake Michigan.

These are but a few recent examples of Chicago's long tradition of urban greening, dating back to the 1909 Burnham and Bennett Plan of Chicago, and nurtured vigorously by such regional NGOs as the Openlands Project.

Many other cities have their own homegrown ecological cities initiatives in progress. For example:

• Manhattan, New York. On Manhattan's West Side, an abandoned elevated rail structure extends 1.5 miles from 34th Street to Greenwich Village. Known as the "High Line," the broad steel structure now supports abundant plant life, described as "an amazing example of a self-seeding self-sustaining urban landscape" with no human contribution to the formation of soil and biodiversity. At the urging of a local NGO, "Friends of the High Line," New York City in 2002 officially began to convert the trestle into a pedestrian greenway traversing one of the most densely built-up districts of the city. An international design competition was held in 2003 to solicit alternative visions for a High Line linear greenway and park (www.thehighline.org).

• New Haven, Connecticut. The "Livable City Initiative" was formed in 1995 as a collaboration between the City of New Haven and the Community Foundation of Greater New Haven to assist neighborhood organizations with the design, planting, and maintenance of community gardens and greenspaces. Closely related is the Urban Resources Initiative (URI) (www.yale.edu/uri) based at the Yale School of Forestry and Environmental Studies. According to the *URI Newsletter*, the initiative's objective is to "foster environmental stewardship and human development in the New Haven area by promoting citizen-based management of natural resources through education, institutional cooperation, and professional guidance." URI and the Livable City Initiative have jointly assisted community groups to convert dozens of vacant tracts in lower-income neighborhoods to flower and vegetable gardens and community mini-parks. . . .

The Challenge of Watersheds

Local urban watersheds, like Pittsburgh's Nine Mile Run, are emerging as important geographic foci of urban ecology efforts in many metropolitan areas. The Ecological Cities Project, under a grant from the National Science Foundation, is studying comparative regional experiences in pursuing multiple environmental, social, and economic goals at the small watershed scale. Typically, metropolitan-scale drainage systems flow from their headwaters in rural areas or suburbs, through lower-income urban districts, past (and sometimes under) central business districts, and then discharge into tidewater, lakes, or larger streams. Along the way, they cross numerous political and property boundaries, thus posing formidable challenges for multijurisdictional cooperation.

Although generalizations are dangerous, the internal diversity of metropolitan watersheds—socioeconomic, political, cultural, and ecological—challenges local activists to promote a "watershed perspective" to engender a more unified approach to problem solving. This perspective may be easier to develop when one or more specific problems—such as flooding, poor water quality, fish kills, shortage of drinking water, or lack of public access—loom large to many of the stakeholders. Once a watershed alliance is organized and possibly incorporated, it may accrue experience, visibility, and credibility. It may then become an ongoing voice for watershed issues not limited to the problem that initially brought it to life.

Such has been the case with the Charles River Watershed Association (www.crwa.org) in the Boston area, formed in the 1960s to promote wetland protection as an alternative to structural flood control. Since its founding, it has addressed issues of water quality, minimum flows, public recreation, and ecological restoration. A similar watershed group is the Houston-area Buffalo Bayou Association, which began primarily to dissuade the Army Corps of Engineers from channelizing the remaining natural streams in the area. Together with the Bayou Preservation Association (another Houston-area group) it recently released a 20-year master plan for the Buffalo Bayou watershed, including extensive greenway and downtown esplanade elements (www.buffalobayou.org). . . .

Urban Ecology Will Benefit Society

One of the potential fringe benefits of watershed restoration and urban ecology activities is the opportunity for social interaction among interested persons from diverse neighbor-hoods, backgrounds, and walks of life. New York University environmental ethicist Andrew Light has identified what he terms "ecological citizenship" that may arise from serendipi-tous contact among volunteers and others cooperating in ecological restoration and advocacy projects. This points to an important dimension of urban ecology strategies: They may relieve the sense of helplessness and loss of community that is a widely lamented attribute of metropolitan growth. While the numerical results of urban ecological activities in terms of trees planted or protected, wetland hectares re-stored, invasive species removed, fish stocks revived, song-birds counted, and bugs discovered by children may be small, the ultimate outcome of such work may be a halo effect of good feelings and a sense of belonging that comes from di-rect personal contact with nature and each other. This may be a key element of social adaptation to life in the enveloping twenty-first century metropolis.

"Large cities are on the front lines of a diversifying national population."

Cities Will Become More Racially and Ethnically Diverse

Alan Berube

The results of Census 2000 indicate that America's urban populations are becoming more diverse, Alan Berube contends in the following viewpoint. According to Berube, the nation's largest cities are experiencing a decline in white population while the percentage of Hispanics, African Americans, and Asian Americans has increased. He concludes that urban governments must take these demographic changes into account when determining how best to provide housing, public education, and other basic services to city residents. Berube is a senior research associate at the Brookings Institution, an independent think tank that conducts research on many topics, including metropolitan policy.

As you read, consider the following questions:
1. According to Berube, what percentage of America's largest cities had majority white populations in 2000?
2. What cities not located on the West Coast experienced growth in their Asian populations, as stated by the author?
3. What does Berube believe will determine the social health of American cities?

Alan Berube, "Racial and Ethnic Change in the Nation's Largest Cities," *Redefining Urban and Suburban America: Evidence from Census 2000, Volume One.* Washington, DC: Brookings Institution Press, 2003. Copyright © 2003 by the Brookings Institution. Reproduced by permission.

The 1990s were a landmark decade in the demographic composition of America's largest cities. Between 1990 and 2000, the largest cities in the United States transitioned from majority white to "majority minority"—that is, whites went from representing more than half to less than half of the overall population of these cities. The transformation was more than marginal: the combined white share of population in the 100 largest cities dropped dramatically, from 52 percent in 1990 to 44 percent in 2000.

The rapid racial and ethnic diversification of city populations represents a magnification of trends in the remainder of the country. Overall, as white share of population in the 100 largest cities declined from 52 percent to 44 percent, its share in the rest of the country dropped by a somewhat smaller degree, from 82 percent to 75 percent. Hispanic share of population rose proportionately in both areas; in the largest cities nearly one in four individuals identified himself/herself as Hispanic, versus one in ten elsewhere. The largest racial/ethnic difference between the top 100 cities and the rest of the nation was in the black population; its share in cities remains almost three times as high as it is elsewhere.

The transformation to minority white population in the largest cities in the 1990s occurred in the aggregate and also in specific cities. In fact, 18 of the top 100 cities saw their white share of population drop from more than 50 percent to less than 50 percent during the decade (table 8-1). These cities were at the forefront of a diversifying nation and include many places in which changes in the racial and ethnic makeup of the population were most dramatic. Anaheim, for instance, experienced the largest decline in white share among the largest 100 cities, from 57 percent of the city's population in 1990 to 36 percent in 2000. Notably there are cities from every area of the country on this list of 18: cities in five states of the South, Milwaukee and St. Louis in the Midwest, Albuquerque and four California cities in the West, and Boston, Rochester, and Philadelphia in the Northeast. None of the 18 cities experienced less than a 7 percent drop in white share of population; even those cities near the bottom of the list still underwent a remarkable shift in a decade's time.

In total, of the largest 100 cities only 52 had majority white populations in 2000, down from 70 in 1990. . . . The cities with the largest minority shares are quite diverse in and among themselves. Some are stagnating or declining cities with traditionally large minority populations, such as Detroit, Birmingham, Miami, and Newark; some are "on the rebound," adding diverse new residents to large existing minority bases, such as Oakland and Jersey City; and others, according to Robert Lang and Patrick A. Simmons, are fast-growing "boomburbs" in traditionally high-immigrant metros, such as Hialeah and Santa Ana.

On the other end of the spectrum, many of the majority-white cities were in the states of the West North Central and Mountain regions. Cities in the nation's agricultural belt, like Des Moines, Lincoln, and Omaha, continue to draw residents from their states' predominantly white populations. None received black residents to the degree that industrial cities of the Northeast and Rust Belt did in the early 1900s, and none today is a magnet for international immigration like New York, Houston, Atlanta, or most cities in California. Mountain state cities like Colorado Springs and Mesa are growing in large part by drawing white population from other parts of the United States.

The Hispanic Population Boom

As in the rest of the nation, Hispanics were the fastest-growing major race/ethnic group in large cities in the 1990s. The boom in their population is owed both to increased immigration from Latin America during a decade of strong economic growth and enhanced job opportunity and to the higher fertility rates that accompany the younger age structure of first- and second-generation Hispanic families. In the nation as a whole, nearly 40 percent of net new residents in the 1990s were Hispanic; the corresponding figure in the largest 100 cities was *more than 80 percent*.

Large increases during the 1990s in the numbers of Hispanics and Asians living in cities occurred alongside continuing declines in the number of white city residents. It was the combination of trends that resulted in the largest cities "tipping" from majority white to majority nonwhite in the 1990s.

A Significant Decline in White Population

The size of the overall decline in white population was not trivial. White population in the top 100 cities combined dropped by 2.3 million people during the decade, or 8.5 percent. Some 71 of these 100 cities experienced a decline in white population of at least 2 percent. . . . Some of this population decline may be related to the introduction of the new multiple-race categories, but the "reclassification" effect is likely to be small.

The phenomenon of white population decrease was widespread among the top 100 cities, but a few large cities dom-

Table 8-1. Eighteen Large Cities That Went from Majority White to Majority Minority During the 1990s

Percent

City	White share 1990	White share 2000	Decline
Anaheim, CA	56.6	35.9	20.8
Riverside, CA	61.3	45.6	15.7
Milwaukee, WI	60.8	45.4	15.4
Rochester, NY	58.3	44.3	14.0
Sacramento, CA	53.4	40.5	12.8
Fort Worth, TX	56.5	45.8	10.7
Augusta-Richmond, GA	54.0	43.7	10.3
Philadelphia, PA	52.1	42.5	9.6
Boston, MA	59.0	49.5	9.5
San Diego, CA	58.7	49.4	9.3
Mobile, AL	58.9	49.8	9.2
Montgomery, AL	56.1	47.1	9.0
Columbus, GA	57.3	48.6	9.0
Norfolk, VA	55.6	47.0	8.5
Albuquerque, NM	58.3	49.9	8.4
Baton Rouge, LA	52.9	44.7	8.1
Shreveport, LA	53.6	45.9	7.7
St. Louis, MO	50.2	42.9	7.3

inated the overall decline. The five largest cities alone—New York, Los Angeles, Chicago, Houston, and Philadelphia—lost nearly 1 million white residents combined, or about 14 percent of their total 1990 white population. As a result, no single racial/ethnic group predominated in those cities in 2000: whites made up one-third of all residents, Hispanics 30 Percent, blacks 25 percent, and Asian/Pacific Islanders 8 percent.

A number of other large cities experienced much faster losses of white residents during the decade than did the five largest cities. In 20 cities white population loss exceeded 20 percent. Cities experiencing the largest declines included predominantly black cities like Detroit (53 percent) and Birmingham (40 percent), as well as cities with a large Hispanic presence like Long Beach (28 percent) and Jersey City (32 percent).

Changes in Various Populations

Across the 100 largest cities, black population grew at a modest 6.4 percent rate in the 1990s, slightly slower than overall population growth in these cities (9 percent). As a result, the black share of population in these cities shrank by a small amount. In 1990 blacks accounted for 24.7 percent of residents in the 100 largest cities; in 2000 they accounted for 24.1 percent.

Despite the overall gain, black population declined during the 1990s in 16 of the 100 largest cities. Of these 16 cities, 8 were in California alone, in high-priced markets such as San Francisco, San Diego, San Jose, and Los Angeles. Other high-cost cities like Atlanta and Washington also lost black residents during the decade, as did older industrial cities like St. Louis, Baltimore, Dayton, and Pittsburgh that experienced significant overall population loss.

The 100 largest cities collectively added 3.8 million Hispanic residents in the 1990s, a dramatic 42.6 percent increase. The typical city witnessed an even larger gain—the median increase in Hispanic population across the 100 cities was 64.5 percent. Gains were widespread: 97 of the cities experienced an increase in Hispanic population, and Hispanic population in 32 cities more than doubled in size.

Ten Texas cities together gained 1 million Hispanics, more than one-fourth of the total gain across all 100 cities. Unlike some other U.S. regions in which Hispanic population increased largely as a result of immigration from Latin America, these Texas cities experienced significant natural increases in Hispanic population. Some 20 percent of Hispanics in the ten large Texas cities were under the age of 10 in 2000 versus 10 percent of non-Hispanic whites.

The rapid gains in Hispanic population that occurred in many cities shifted the ethnic makeup of their resident populations rather dramatically, particularly in cities in the Southwest and West. Hispanic share of population in the top 100 cities overall increased 5 percentage points in the 1990s, but 12 of the top 100 cities saw their Hispanic share of population increase by at least 10 percentage points. In Phoenix, for instance, where one in five residents was Hispanic in 1990, more than one in three was in 2000.

Like the black population, Asians represented roughly the same proportion of overall population in the 100 largest cities at the end of the decade (6.6 percent) as they did at the beginning (5.2 percent). But the small change in share masked a significant increase in this population's growth in the 1990s in large cities—38.3 percent overall, a net increase of more than 1 million Asian residents.

As with Hispanic population, gains in Asian population were widespread: 95 of the top 100 cities experienced increases. But gains tended to be somewhat smaller than Hispanic gains: only 11 cities underwent a doubling (or more) of their Asian populations. Interestingly, growth centers for Asian population could be found outside of the traditional West Coast magnets for Asian immigration: Garland, Jersey City, New York, and St. Paul all saw their Asian population shares increase by at least 3 percentage points during the decade.

The rapid rise in large-city Hispanic and Asian populations should not overshadow the fact that on the whole, their numbers actually grew faster during the 1990s in areas outside the 100 largest cities. The 100-city growth rates for Hispanics and Asians were 43 percent and 38 percent respectively; outside the 100 cities, their growth rates were 68 percent and 58 percent. Black population registered a 24 percent increase outside the largest cities, compared with only 6 percent within the cities. According to Alan Berube and William H. Frey, these differences reflect the overall trend of faster suburban than city growth in the 1990s and the fact that minority populations in increasing numbers are choosing smaller cities and suburbs. Nevertheless, the rapid rise of minority populations in cities is of particular interest given that it occurred alongside white population loss and was the underlying reason for the shift to a "majority minority" population in the largest cities in 2000. . . .

How Cities Should Respond

This [viewpoint] demonstrates that large cities are on the front lines of a diversifying national population. Across all 100 cities considered for analysis, there appeared a consistent pattern of decreasing white population, rapidly growing Hispanic and Asian population, and modestly increasing black population.

The rapid diversification of city populations during the last decade has implications for the economic, social, and political climate of these places. Cities that grew the fastest were those that attracted new residents from all racial/ethnic populations. This finding suggests that cities hoping to achieve real growth need to provide a living environment attractive to families of varying race and ethnicity. A renewed focus on basic services like schools, safety, and infrastructure that benefit city residents in a broad way may be the approach most likely to appeal to households across the racial/ethnic spectrum.

In thinking about basic services such as these, cities will need to understand the unique characteristics of their resident populations and how the changing populations change specific services needs. In Aurora, Colorado, for instance, where one out of every fifteen residents in 1990 was Hispanic, now one out of every five is Hispanic. Large demographic shifts at the city level such as this are likely to affect the structure and delivery of services such as health care, public education, housing, and public transportation. These shifts may also affect cities' fiscal capacities and thus their ability to pay for these services. Understanding the context at the local level, through continued analysis of Census 2000 data, can help individual cities respond to change as well as anticipate future needs.

Despite increasing diversity at the city level, people of different races and ethnicities continue to live apart in many cities in the United States. In Washington, D.C., for instance, more than three-fourths of the black population lives in neighborhoods that are at least 80 percent black. No single racial/ethnic group makes up a majority of the population in Los Angeles, but the student population in the LA Unified School District is 71 percent Hispanic. The social health of cities may rest in large part with how racial and ethnic diversity plays out at the neighborhood level. Researchers have begun to study this question with Census 2000 short-form data, and the socioeconomic data available from the long form will provide additional opportunities to examine diversity in all its aspects.

"The lines between cities and non-cities are blurring, and the longer our economic boom continues, the more the lines will blur."

Cities Will Begin to Resemble Suburbs

Fred Siegel

In the following viewpoint Fred Siegel opines that as suburbs are becoming more economically powerful than neighboring urban areas, American cities are beginning to take on aspects of suburbia. He contends that this transformation of cities includes features such as big-box stores and suburban-style homes with backyards. According to Siegel, successful urban mayors are adapting to this new type of city and developing policies that help increase job growth and aid the transformation of empty lots into green space and suburban-style, single-family home developments. Siegel is a professor of history at the Cooper Union for the Advancement of Science and Art in New York City.

As you read, consider the following questions:
1. Where is Pennsylvania's leading industrial center, according to Siegel?
2. According to the mayor of Denver, what is the role of urban mayors?
3. What prediction of H.G. Wells does Siegel say is coming true?

Fred Siegel, "America's Startling New Urban Geography," *The American Enterprise*, vol. 11, July 2000, p. 40. Copyright © 2000 by the American Enterprise Institute for Public Policy Research. Reproduced by permission of *The American Enterprise*, a magazine of Politics, Business, and Culture. On the Web at www.TAEmag.com.

In 1902, H.G. Wells wrote, "Already for a great number of businesses it is no longer necessary that the office should be in London, and only habit, tradition, and minor consideration keep them there." By the telephone and the post office parcel service "almost all the labor of ordinary shopping can be avoided. . . . The mistress of the house has all her local tradesmen, all the great London shops, the circulating library, theater box-office, the post-office and cab-rank, the nurse inst. and the doctor within reach of her hand." Wells was prescient to see a hundred years ago that new technologies would disperse across the landscape the amenities once available only to city dwellers. The United States is decentralizing faster than any other society in history. Fifteen of the largest 25 cities have lost 4 million people since 1965, while the nation's total population has risen by 60 million. But at the same time that the large "vertical cities" have lost population, mid-sized horizontal cities, better adapted to the automobile and better able to offer a quality of life comparable to the suburbs, have grown rapidly.

Suburbs Are Emerging

In the age of horizontal high-tech cities, Austin now has a larger population than Boston, while Denver, once a provincial mining and oil town, has emerged, thanks to the cable industry, as a major metropolis. If Austin is now larger than Boston, that is because the high-tech economy has created more new jobs in Texas over the past two years than in the entire oil and gas extraction industry.

On the conventional map of America left over from the urban age, the city of Baltimore—home of glorious Camden Yards and the Orioles—looms large in its region. In fact Baltimore is now only the fourth-largest political jurisdiction in Maryland; high-tech Montgomery County on the outskirts of Washington, D.C., has both more jobs and more people. Similarly, San Francisco has become something of a suburb to Silicon Valley. It is now the second-largest city in the Bay Area, with 300,000 fewer people than San Jose and fewer than 50 of the Bay Area's 500 largest public companies. In Northern Virginia, suburban Fairfax County is now home to nearly a million people, and possesess over twice the office space of downtown Boston, Philadelphia, Houston, Denver, Dallas, or Seattle. In fact, it has more office space than all but four of America's cities.

Let's take a look at Philadelphia and its suburbs: The leading industrial center in Pennsylvania is not Pittsburgh or Philadelphia but Montgomery County in suburban Philly. Its 725,000 citizens on the edge of Philadelphia make it more populous than five states, and also give it the highest per-capital income in the state. Its 500,000 jobs (up from 387,000 in 1990) draw in 250,000 commuters daily from as far away as Allentown and Reading—it's like a dispersed center city. Montgomery together with Chester County to its east are now the economic engines of the region. Together they have not only a larger population than Philly but 110,000 more private-sector jobs. Or as William H. Fulton, executive director of the Chester County Planning Commission, puts it, "There's a lot of people out here who don't like to hear that Chester County is a suburb of Philadelphia."

Not only has Philly's western suburban economy surpassed that of its big-city neighbor to the east, but employment in these towns now exceeds the total in major metropolitan areas like New Orleans, Memphis, Buffalo, and Richmond. The western Philadelphia suburbs are actually a bigger economy than several states, including Alaska, Delaware, Montana, North Dakota, South Dakota, Rhode Island, Vermont, and Wyoming. And yet this dispersed collection of towns like Blue Bell, Fort Washington, Plymouth Meeting, the Main Line, Conshohocken, Horsham, Willow Grove, Valley Forge, Jenkintown, King of Prussia, and the Route 202 corridor has no name. Monikers like Silicon Valley Forge, Philacon Valley, Silicon East, and so forth have been thrown out, but not surprisingly in an area that defines itself by dispersal, none of them has stuck.

Creating Suburbs Within Cities

At the same time, Philadelphia proper, outside of its most central core, has been moving in what might be called a semi-suburban direction. Philadelphia has lost 150,000 people over the past decade, and its leaders, particularly the new mayor John Street, have decided to accept the fact that given the lack of immigration to Philly, it is time to plan for a much-shrunken city. He proposes to take advantage of the city's 31,000 empty lots by razing hundreds of empty factories and thousands of empty row houses in order to clear vast swaths of land for new private-sector developers. They would be encouraged to put up suburban-style homes, office buildings, big-box stores—maybe even movie theaters, golf courses, and environmental sanctuaries. "This is," Street says, "a once-in-a-lifetime opportunity. It's the greening of Philadelphia."

This development of a suburb inside a city is already occurring, albeit on a far smaller scale, in one section of Chicago: a landscape of detached houses being built around the Lake Park Pointe shopping center in poverty-stricken Kenwood, near the lake just north of the University of Chicago. Commercially the area is anchored by a huge supermarket, which has already helped raise real-estate values. Meanwhile Chicago is in the process of de-densifying itself by tearing down its public housing high-rises and resheltering the tenants with scatter-site low-rises in a city with plenty of available space—since it has about 1 million fewer people now than it did 30 years ago. Chicago has fewer people but more trees thanks to Mayor [Richard] Daley, who has been planting them everywhere he can, including on rooftops, as a way of both beautifying the city and reducing summer heat.

Similarly, when Baltimore demolished Lafayette Court, a public housing high-rise, it built air-conditioned two-story houses clustered along cul-de-sacs, just like the suburban dream. Asked why, Mayor [Kurt] Schmoke answered, "People didn't want three-story houses. They wanted two-story houses with modern conveniences—and yards."

The Denver Model

Older, sometimes shrinking cities want not only suburban housing; they want the dot.com jobs that first took hold on the periphery, and they're getting them in dozens of places, from the graphic arts districts of Brooklyn to San Francisco's Mission district, where the Yuppie Eradication Project is fighting the rising tide of prosperity by scraping keys on the shiny finish of BMWs owned by the dot.com class enemy.

Mayors across the United States are adapting to this new world in which cities that aren't well managed will have a difficult time competing for the intellectual capital that drives the emerging economy. Mayor Wellington Webb of Denver represents the new model. Under the old model that held sway from the mid-1960s to the early 1990s, urban policy was characterized by what might be called the success of failure. In that mode, the worse a city did, the more it was entitled to ask for from the federal government.

Suburbs Are Resembling Cities

Curiously, at the same time [New York City] is becoming more suburban, the suburbs are becoming more citylike. Back in the days when arugula was to be found only at Balducci's and lattes at little cafes in the Village, food in the suburbs meant white bread. Now, with gourmet food shops everywhere and Starbucks having made its way even to the local mall, no bridges or tunnels need be crossed to satisfy more sophisticated cravings. Indeed, these cravings are now mainstream. Everything is available everywhere. And it's not just food. The *New York Times* reported that a woman in Scarsdale built a successful transportation business shuttling children from school to lessons and sports activities; it seems suburban mothers are now too busy to handle this sort of chore themselves. The notion of hiring someone to shuttle your children about is precisely the kind of thing that would have driven suburban mothers to sneer at Manhattan pretension a few years ago. In the age of ambiguous city-suburban identity, it plays just fine.

Paul Goldberger, *Metropolis Magazine*, March 2001.

Webb is different. An enormously popular African-American Democrat, Webb speaks in a manner that would have been unthinkable a decade ago. He describes mayors as the "CEOs of our cities" whose task it is to "run our cities like private businesses but with a public mission." He has called on mayors to look to business and the new high-tech economy, not Washington, for municipal sustenance. The key to high tech, he argues, is to create the quality of life that will attract the Dilberts of the world, with parks, recreation facilities, etc. And so Philly is trying to hold on to Wharton grads, while Rochester is discovering it needs more cafes.

Webb argues that these city CEOs "need to bury forever the old image of mayors with a tin cup and an extended palm asking for handouts to sustain and expand cumbersome bureaucracies." Rather than looking to the federal government as the salvation of the cities, Webb, like Mayor Daley before him, sees Washington's unfunded mandates and rigid policies, which often serve to subvert suburban development, [as] as much a hindrance as a help. "Congress," he says, "is like an air force which drops laws on cities without looking at the collateral damage." How much of the agenda laid out by Mayor Webb will be firmly institutionalized? George Musgrove, Oakland's deputy city manager, takes the positive view: "A movement of good government for cities has swept the country, and all good mayors—African-American, white, Latino—are governing that way." Musgrove is on to something; New York's success in reducing crime has forced Baltimore to reconsider how it does business. Baltimore, the favorite playpen for Washington policy people, is the site of every known public or private social program—and yet Sandtown-Winchester, recipient of enormous resources and long touted as an example of successful community development, is now recognized to be a failure: There are no stores to speak of in that crime- and fear-ridden neighborhood. The best social program in poor city districts, in short, is crime control; cities that reduce crime and the fear of crime have experienced a revival of the retail districts essential for vibrant neighborhoods.

But while the fresh outlooks represented by new leaders like Wellington Webb make a return to old-style mayors unlikely, there are reasons to worry about how much further reform will go. The improvements in city governance over the past decade are, as a recent study by Syracuse University's Maxwell School points out, largely a function of strong, effective mayors. What happens if their successes aren't institutionalized, if their successors are not so talented?

Blurring Boundaries

That's what was on [former New York mayor] Rudy Giuliani's mind when he gave his State of the City speech [in 2000]. . . . Giuliani, perhaps the most successful of the reform mayors, warned again and again against allowing the city to slide back into the sad shape it had once been in: "Don't turn it back. . . . We blocked the genius of America for the poorest people in New York.". . .

Big cities, rather than being separate cultures, are increasingly home to one phase of life, a place you go when you're young and single and looking to make it in the world. The lines between cities and non-cities are blurring, and the longer our economic boom continues, the more the lines will blur. Exurban populations are recoiling from their exploding growth and increasingly pushing for slower growth and open-space purchases. The effect will be to push new jobs either further out beyond the growth boundaries or, as is increasingly the case, back into the cities where semi-reformed governments, unlike in the 1980s, are now capable of attracting and absorbing growth.

H.G. Wells' prediction is coming true: "The city will diffuse itself until it has taken up considerable areas and many of the characteristics . . . of what is now country, [and] the country will take to itself many of the qualities of the city. The old antithesis will, indeed, cease."

As the boundaries between older, de-densified cities and the dispersed cities of their surrounding counties blur, there are bound to be bitter fights between those who want the new hybrid areas to remain suburban, and those who want more city-like forms in order to curb sprawl and congestion. The great political question for the future is whether this will re-create the kinds of old centralized governments that ultimately did in traditional cities—the very governments that today's exurbanites fled from.

Periodical Bibliography

The following articles have been selected to supplement the diverse views presented in this chapter.

Philip Bess	"Design Matters," *Christian Century*, April 19, 2003.
John Charles	"Managing Urban Growth," *World & I*, August 2000.
Howard Frumkin	"Urban Sprawl and Public Health," *Public Health Reports*, May/June 2002.
Peter Gordon	"Defending Suburban Sprawl," *Public Interest*, Spring 2000.
Roberta Brandes Gratz	"Preserving the Urban Dynamic," *Nation*, April 23, 2001.
C.C. Kraemer	"Beware 'New Urbanism,'" *Freeman*, October 2002.
Catesby Leigh	"It Takes a Village," *National Review*, July 14, 2003.
William L. Nolan	"Urban Growth Too Much of a Good Thing?" *Better Homes and Gardens*, April 2001.
Henry Overman	"The Future of Cities?" *Economic Review*, September 2002.
Vincent Scully	"The American City in A.D. 2025," *Brookings Review*, Summer 2000.
Fred Siegel	"The Death and Life of America's Cities," *Public Interest*, Summer 2002.
Sierra	"Why Shrinking Cities Sprawl," May/June 2002.
Janet Ward	"Back to the Future," *American City & County*, March 2002.

For Further Discussion

Chapter 1

1. The authors in this chapter address several of the problems facing urban America. Which of those problems do you believe deserves the greatest attention? In addition, what problems not discussed in this chapter do you think most seriously affect American cities? Explain your answers.

2. The viewpoints by Charles C. Euchner and Stephen J. McGovern, and by G. Thomas Kingsley and Kathryn L.S. Pettit use statistics to support their views on urban poverty. Whose use of statistics do you find more convincing and why?

3. David Hilfiker contends that the urban poor suffer disproportionately from health problems. Assuming his argument is valid, what steps would you take to improve health care in American cities?

Chapter 2

1. Margery Austin Turner and her coauthors argue in favor of HOPE VI, while Paul A. Cleveland and R. Chris Frohock assert that it is a failed public housing program. Whose argument do you find more convincing? In addition, do you believe public housing programs in general are beneficial to urban America, or do you feel that other programs, such as loans that make it easier for inner-city families to buy homes, would better improve the housing situation in American cities? Explain your answers, citing from the viewpoints and other relevant sources.

2. Jared Bernstein and Jeff Chapman are an economist and economic analyst, respectively, while Carl F. Horowitz is an expert on labor issues and urban affairs policy. Given their careers, which authors do you think are better able to interpret the effects of living wages on urban workers? Why? If you agree with Bernstein and Chapman, how would you try to fulfill the goals of the living wage movement? If you believe that Horowitz's interpretation is more accurate, what steps, if any, would you take to improve the economic conditions of urban workers? Please explain your answers.

3. Wendell Cox contends that the transit problems of urban workers could be solved by providing them with cars. However, he does not address the issues that affect city driving, such as traffic and a shortage of parking spaces. Given those omissions from his viewpoint, do you think Cox's solution is realistic? How would

you address those caveats while keeping his answer viable? Explain your answers.

Chapter 3

1. Andra J. Bannister, David L. Carter, and Joseph Schafer assert that curfews can be successful if combined with other programs. Do you believe the afterschool programs detailed by Georgia Hall, Laura Israel, and Joyce Shortt could pair effectively with juvenile curfews? Why or why not?

2. Paul E. Peterson and Barbara Miner disagree on the effects of voucher programs. Whose argument do you find more convincing and why? If you agree with Peterson, what do you believe is the best way to bring vouchers to more American cities? If you agree with Miner, what steps would you take to improve the quality of education in urban public schools?

3. The authors in this chapter focus largely on the roles that schools and government can play in improving the lives of urban youth. Where do you believe parents fit into this equation? Explain your answer.

Chapter 4

1. After reading the viewpoints both in this chapter and in the other chapters, do you believe Americans should be hopeful or concerned about the future of their cities? What elements of urban life do you think will be most problematic, and which do you believe will most likely improve in the coming decades? Please explain your answer, using material from the book.

2. John Fregonese and Lynn Peterson have backgrounds in urban planning while Randal O'Toole is an economist. Which of them is better qualified to address the effects smart-growth policies may have on urban America? Why?

3. Alan Berube posits that American cities are becoming more diverse, in part because of immigration. What are some of the changes, both positive and negative, that you believe a growing immigrant population will bring to the nation's metropolises? Explain your answers.

Organizations to Contact

The editors have compiled the following list of organizations concerned with the issues debated in this book. The descriptions are derived from materials provided by the organizations. All have publications or information available for interested readers. The list was compiled on the date of publication of the present volume; the information provided here may change. Be aware that many organizations take several weeks or longer to respond to inquiries, so allow as much time as possible.

Brookings Institution Metropolitan Policy Program
1775 Massachusetts Ave. NW, Washington, DC 20036
(202) 797-6139 • fax: (202) 797-2965
e-mail: urbancenter@brookings.edu
Web site: www.brookings.edu

The Brookings Institution is an organization that researches and analyzes topics such as economics and governance. Its Metropolitan Policy Program provides decision makers with information on the challenges facing American cities. Publications available on the Web site include *A Progressive Agenda for Metropolitan America* and *Smart Growth: The Future of the American Metropolis?*

Cato Institute
1000 Massachusetts Ave. NW, Washington, DC 20001-5403
(202) 842-0200 • fax: (202) 842-3490
e-mail: cato@cato.org • Web site: www.cato.org

The Cato Institute is a libertarian public policy research foundation that aims to limit the role of government and protect civil liberties. Its Web site offers a number of publications on education, smart growth, wages, and other urban issues, including "Critiquing Sprawl's Critics," and "School Choice in the District of Columbia: Saving Taxpayers Money, Increasing Opportunities for Children."

Congress for the New Urbanism (CNU)
Marquette Building, 140 S. Dearborn Ave., Suite 310, Chicago, IL 60603
(312) 551-7300 • fax: (312) 346-3323
e-mail: cnuinfo@cnu.org • Web site: www.cnu.org

CNU is a nonprofit organization that teaches architects, developers, and others involved in the creation of cities the principles of New Urbanism. Among these principles are walkable neighborhoods and pleasant civic spaces. Its publications include newsletters, reports, and educational materials.

Employment Policies Institute
1775 Pennsylvania Ave. NW, Suite 1200, Washington, DC
20006-4605 • (202) 463-7650 • fax: (202) 463-7107
e-mail: info@epionline.org • Web site: www.epionline.org

The Employment Policies Institute is a research organization that studies issues affecting entry-level employment and employment growth. The institute, which sponsors research conducted by independent economists, opposes minimum-wage and living-wage policies. Publications available from the Web site include *Raising New York's Minimum Wage: A Poor Way to Help the Working Poor* and *Living Wage and Earned Income Tax Credit: A Comparative Analysis*.

Enterprise Foundation
10227 Wincopin Circle, Suite 500, Columbia, MD 21044
(800) 624-4298 • fax: (410) 964-1918
e-mail: mail@enterprisefoundation.org
Web site: www.enterprisefoundation.org

The Enterprise Foundation aids community developers by providing them with the tools they need to improve their cities, including consulting, training, and fundraising. Congressional testimony on issues such as housing can be found on the Web site, while other publications can be ordered.

National Coalition for the Homeless
1012 Fourteenth St. NW, #600, Washington, DC 20005-3471
(202) 737-6444 • fax: (202) 737-6445
e-mail: info@nationalhomeless.org
Web site: www.nationalhomeless.org

The National Coalition uses public education, policy advocacy, and grassroots organizing to fulfill its goal of ending homelessness. Its work focuses on the areas of housing justice, economic justice, health care justice, and civil and voting rights. Factsheets, reports, and information on legislation relating to the homeless are available on the Web site.

National League of Cities
1301 Pennsylvania Ave. NW, Suite 550, Washington, DC 20004
(202) 626-3000 • fax: (202) 626-3043
e-mail: inet@nlc.org • Web site: www.nlc.org

The National League of Cities is an organization that represents municipal governments throughout the United States and aims to promote cities as centers of opportunity and leadership. Publications that can be purchased from the Web site include "City Voices, Children's Needs" and "Major Factors Affecting America's Cities."

National Urban League
120 Wall St., New York, NY 10005
(212) 558-5300 • fax: (212) 344-5332
e-mail: info@nul.org • Web site: www.nul.org
The National Urban League is a community-based movement
that helps African Americans improve their economic and social
power. The league's publications include reports, studies, *Opportunity Journal*, annual reports, and the *National Urban League Institute of Opportunity & Equality Fact Book.*

Poverty & Race Research Action Council (PRRAC)
3000 Connecticut Ave. NW, Suite 200, Washington, DC 20008
(202) 387-9887 • fax: (202) 387-0764
e-mail: info@prrac.org • Web site: www.prrac.org
PRRAC is a not-for-profit organization whose mission is to create
and distribute research on the relationship between race and
poverty, promote policies that alleviate conditions caused by that
relationship, and support social science research on those topics.
Its newsletter *Poverty & Race* is published six times per year, and
handbooks and anthologies can be ordered from the Web site.

Progressive Policy Institute
600 Pennsylvania Ave. SE, Suite 400, Washington, DC 20003
(202) 547-0001 • fax: (202) 544-5014
Web site: www.ppionline.org
The Progressive Policy Institute is a research and education institute that aims to define and promote a new progressive politics for
the United States. A variety of publications is available on the Web
site, including e-mail newsletters, policy briefings and reports, and
the journal *Blueprint: Ideas for a New Century.*

Thoreau Institute
PO Box 1590, Bandon, OR 97411
(541) 347-1517
e-mail: rot@ti.org • Web site: www.ti.org
The Thoreau Institute seeks ways to protect the environment
without regulation, bureaucracy, or central control. The institute,
which is critical of smart-growth policies and mass transit, helps
environmentalists and state and local groups understand and influence public land management. Publications can be ordered from
the Web site.

Urban Institute
2100 M St. NW, Washington, DC 20037
(202) 833-7200
e-mail: paffairs@ui.urban.org • Web site: www.urban.org
The Urban Institute is a nonprofit educational and research organization that examines social, political, and economic problems. The institute also provides information to decision makers to help them address those issues. The Web site features publications on many urban issues, including crime, education, and welfare reform.

U.S. Conference of Mayors
1620 I St. NW, Washington, DC 20006
(202) 293-7330 • fax: (202) 293-2352
e-mail: jwelfley@usmayors.org
Web site: www.usmayors.org
The U.S. Conference of Mayors is the official nonpartisan organization of cities with populations of thirty thousand or more. Its roles include providing mayors with management tools, improving the relationship between federal and municipal governments, and creating a forum where mayors can exchange ideas. Press releases and Web casts are available on the Web site.

Web Sites

PLANetizen
e-mail: info@planetizen.com • Web site: www.planetizen.com
PLANetizen is a Web site that provides information for people involved in urban planning and development. The site features news, an e-mail newsletter, and commentary on issues such as transportation, smart growth, and housing.

UrbanFutures.Org
e-mail: feedback@reason.org • Web site: www.urbanfutures.org
A product of the Reason Foundation, the Urban Futures Program supports research on issues such as urban growth and revitalizing America's inner cities and promotes market-oriented solutions to urban problems. Policy studies, speeches, and commentary are available on the Web site.

Bibliography of Books

Jonathan Barnett   *Redesigning Cities: Principles, Practice, Implementation.* Chicago: Planners Press, 2003.

Steve Belmont   *Cities in Full: Recognizing and Realizing the Great Potential of Urban America.* Chicago: Planners Press, 2002.

Martha Burr et al.   *Helping America's Homeless: Emergency Shelter or Affordable Housing.* Washington, DC: Urban Institute Press, 2001.

Sean Donahue   *Gangs: Stories of Life and Death from the Streets.* New York: Thunder's Mouth, 2002.

Andres Duany, Elizabeth Plater-Zyberk, and Jeff Speck   *Suburban Nation: The Rise of Sprawl and the Decline of the American Dream.* New York: North Point Press, 2000.

Charles C. Euchner and Stephen J. McGovern   *Urban Policy Reconsidered: Dialogues on the Problems and Prospects of American Cities.* New York: Routledge, 2003.

Owen Fiss   *A Way Out: America's Ghettos and the Legacy of Racism.* Princeton, NJ: Princeton University Press, 2003.

Jonathan L. Gifford   *Flexible Urban Transportation.* New York: Pergamon, 2003.

Edward G. Goetz   *Clearing the Way: Deconcentrating the Poor in Urban America.* Washington, DC: Urban Institute Press, 2003.

Harry Gold   *Urban Life and Society.* Upper Saddle River, NJ: Prentice-Hall, 2002.

Stephen Goldsmith   *Putting Faith in Neighborhoods: Making Cities Work Through Grassroots Citizenship.* Noblesville, IN: Hudson Institute, 2002.

Paul S. Grogan and Tony Proscio   *Comeback Cities: A Blueprint for Urban Neighborhood Revival.* Boulder, CO: Westview Press, 2000.

Owen D. Gutfreund   *Twentieth-Century Sprawl: Highways and the Reshaping of the American Landscape.* New York: Oxford University Press, 2004.

Gwendolyn Hallsmith   *The Key to Sustainable Cities: Meeting Human Needs, Transforming Community Systems.* Gabriola Island, Canada: New Society Publishers, 2003.

George Hazel and Roger Parry   *Making Cities Work.* New York: Wiley-Academy, 2004.

David Hilfiker   *Urban Injustice: How Ghettos Happen.* New York:
                         Seven Stories Press, 2002.

Alison Isenberg   *Downtown America: A History of the Place and the
                         People Who Made It.* Chicago: University of
                         Chicago Press, 2004.

Bruce Katz and   *Redefining Urban and Suburban America:
Robert E. Lang, eds.   Evidence from Census 2000.* Vol. 1. Washington,
                         DC: Brookings Institution Press, 2003.

Kenneth Kolson   *Big Plans: The Allure and Folly of Urban Design.*
                         Baltimore: Johns Hopkins University Press,
                         2001.

Mike Males   *Kids and Guns: How Politicians, Experts, and the
                         Press Fabricate the Fear of Youth.* Monroe, ME:
                         Common Courage Press, 2000, updated by
                         author 2004.

Martin V. Melosi   *Effluent America: Cities, Industry, Energy, and the
                         Environment.* Pittsburgh: University of Pitts-
                         burgh Press, 2001.

Katherine S. Newman   *A Different Shade of Gray: Midlife and Beyond in
                         the Inner City.* New York: New Press, 2003.

Katherine S. Newman   *No Shame in My Game: The Working Poor in the
                         Inner City.* New York: Vintage Books, 2000.

Pietro S. Nivola   *Tense Commandments: Federal Prescriptions and
                         City Problems.* Washington, DC: Brookings
                         Institution Press, 2002.

Dom Nozzi   *Road to Ruin: An Introduction to Sprawl and How
                         to Cure It.* Westport, CT: Praeger, 2003.

Randal O'Toole   *The Vanishing Automobile and Other Urban
                         Myths: How Smart Growth Will Harm American
                         Cities.* Bandon, OR: Thoreau Institute, 2001.

Mary Anne Pitman   *Caring as Tenacity: Stories of Urban School
and Debbie Zorn, eds.   Survival.* Crosskill, NJ: Hampton Press, 2003.

Sol Stern   *Breaking Free: Public School Lessons and the Imper-
                         ative of School Choice.* San Francisco: Encounter
                         Books, 2003.

Alexander von Hoffman   *House by House, Block by Block: The Rebirth of
                         America's Urban Neighborhoods.* New York:
                         Oxford University Press, 2003.

Index